Praise for **AN[...]**

"And No Birds Sa[...]
evocation of the fire tha[...]
ranks as one of Mowat's [...]
MORDECAI RICHLER

"Mowat's finest work."
TIME MAGAZINE

"One of the things we learn about Mowat is that he's damned
lucky to be alive. He had so many brushes with death
that it began to seem as though he had a charmed life. This
experience may explain a lot about Mowat's postwar career,
when he became an anti-establishment hell-raiser as a writer."
WILLIAM FRENCH, GLOBE AND MAIL

"In battle scenes of searing immediacy and resonating
insights, Farley Mowat conveys the immense toll war wages
on men's psyches as they are thrown into suicidal situations
by a sacrificial high command. There is humor, too,
some of it hilarious, and poignancy, both contributing to an
intensity of feeling that fuels a powerful narrative drive."
PUBLISHERS WEEKLY

"The battle parlance and terminology in this book
are utterly authentic. Every line rings true . . . Farley Mowat
was a good soldier and he has written a good book."
THE GAZETTE (Montreal)

"The reader is swept up by the vivid accounts of death and con-
flict among men becoming soldiers in the crucible of combat."
QUILL & QUIRE

AND NO BIRDS SANG

FARLEY MOWAT

Douglas & McIntyre

For Claire and Helen,
and for all those others who
endured the aftermath.

. . . .

Copyright © 2012 by Farley Mowat Limited
Originally published in 1975

23 24   9   8

All rights reserved. No part of this book may be reproduced,
stored in a retrieval system or transmitted, in any form
or by any means, without the prior written consent of the
publisher or a licence from The Canadian Copyright Licensing
Agency (Access Copyright). For a copyright licence,
visit www.accesscopyright.ca or call toll free to 1-800-893-5777.

Douglas and McIntyre (2013) Ltd.
P.O. Box 219, Madeira Park
British Columbia, Canada V0N 2H0
www.douglas-mcintyre.com

Cataloguing data available from Library and Archives Canada
ISBN 978-1-77100-030-7
ISBN 978-1-77100-031-4 (ebook)

Cover and text design by Jessica Sullivan
Cover illustration by Brian Tong
Printed and bound in Canada by Friesens
Distributed in the U.S. by Publishers Group West

We gratefully acknowledge the financial support
of the Canada Council for the Arts, the British Columbia Arts
Council, the Province of British Columbia through the
Book Publishing Tax Credit and the Government of Canada
through the Canada Book Fund for our publishing activities.

O what can ail thee, Knight at arms,
Alone and palely loitering?
The sedge has withered from the Lake,
And no birds sing!

JOHN KEATS
"LA BELLE DAME SANS MERCI"

War was return of earth to ugly earth,
War was foundering of sublimities,
Extinction of each happy art and faith
By which the world had still kept head in air,
Protesting logic or protesting love,
Until the unendurable moment struck—
The inward scream, the duty to run mad.

ROBERT GRAVES
"RECALLING WAR"

PART I

My friend, you would not tell with such high zest

To children ardent for some desperate glory,

The old Lie: Dulce et decorum est

Pro patria mori.*

WILFRED OWEN "DULCE ET DECORUM EST"

*It is sweet and proper to die for one's fatherland.

ON THE SECOND DAY OF September, 1939, I was painting the porch of our clapboard house in the rural Ontario town of Richmond Hill when my father pulled into the driveway at the helm of his red convertible. He looked as if he might have had a drink or two—high-coloured and exhilarated.

"Farley, my lad, there's bloody big news! The war is on! Nothing official yet, but the Regiment's been ordered to mobilize, and I'm to go back in with the rank of major, bum arm and all. There'll be a place for you too. You'll have to sweat a bit for it, of course, but if you keep your nose clean and work like hell there'll be the King's Commission."

He spoke as if he was offering me a knighthood or, at the very least, membership in some exceedingly exclusive order.

Slim, wiry and sharply handsome, my father still carried himself like the young soldier who had gone off in 1915 to fight in the Great War, fired by the ideals of Empire—a Soldier of the King—one of those gay young men whose sense of right, of chivalry, was to bait them into the uttermost reaches of hell. Although he had come back from Hades with his right arm made useless by German bullets, he nevertheless remained an impassioned supporter of the peacetime volunteer militia, and in particular of his own outfit, the Hastings and Prince Edward Regiment, an infantry unit composed of countrymen and townsmen from southeastern Ontario, which was familiarly if inelegantly known as the Hasty Pees.

My father's news excited me tremendously for I had long been inflamed by his fulminations against the Russophobe French, British and U.S. politicians and industrialists who had connived at the growth and spread of fascism, concealing their real admiration for it beneath the public explanation that it was the only trustworthy "bulwark against communism." I shared my father's conviction that these men had betrayed democracy and I took the debacle of Munich and the sell-out of Czechoslovakia as proof of this. I believed that every healthy young man in the freedom-espousing countries was duty bound to take up arms against the Fascist plague and, in particular, the singularly bestial German brand.

Nevertheless I had no great inclination to follow my father into the tightly disciplined ranks of the infantry. The kind of independent derring-do which appealed to me seemed best to be found in the fighter arm of the Air Force.

Early in October I presented myself at a Royal Canadian Air Force recruiting station in Toronto... together with, it seemed, about half the male population of that city. When I finally stood before a harassed recruiting sergeant, he gave me short shrift.

"The Air Force don't need no peach-faced kids," he told me with disdain. "Shove off! You're in the way!"

In truth, I looked much younger and more fragile than I was. The year I turned ten, and looked a delicate six, my mother was concerned enough to take me to a famous pediatrician—a gruff old man who checked me over, then snorted in some irritation at my mother:

"If you'd wanted a football player for a son, you should have got yourself sired by a wrestler... and married a truck driver."

In public school I was the Shrimp, and in high school it was Baby Face. Unable to compete physically with my peers, I grew up as an essentially solitary youth who, like Kipling's Cat, preferred to walk by his lone. Most of my free time was spent wandering the fields and woods, for I was an avid naturalist. By the time I was thirteen, in Saskatchewan where we were then living, I was traipsing off alone on thirty-mile snowshoe trips across the frozen plains, sleeping out in haystacks at twenty below zero, and all for the glimpse of a snowy owl or a flock of prairie chickens. Peach-faced I may have been but, appearances to the contrary, I was no sickly kid.

The sergeant was waiting impatiently for me to leave; instead, I pulled out my birth certificate. He glanced at it dubiously.

"Eighteen, eh? Hmmmm. But you still can't go for air crew. Too young, and anyway we got a waiting list ten miles long. You might come back in about six months."

So, on May 12, 1940, the day after my nineteenth birthday, I returned to the recruiting station and was grudgingly allowed to take a medical. The Air Force doctors could find nothing to fault me with except that I weighed four pounds less than the official minimum. That was enough to fail me. It was: Goodbye, Mr. Mowat, and thanks for trying.

I seethed with fury all during the train trip home to Richmond Hill.

"What do they need pilots built like King Kong *for?*" I demanded bitterly of my father that night. "They figure I might personally have to belt Hitler on the snoot?"

He soothed me with derogatory remarks about the elitist pretensions of the "junior service," then cunningly reminded me that there were still openings for officer candidates in the 2nd Battalion (the militia battalion) of the Hasty Pees.

Since there now seemed nothing else for it, I was persuaded to take an army medical. Before weighing me the elderly examining doctor, a good friend of my father's, sent me off to drink as much water as I could hold. Well ballasted and gurgling like an over-full bathtub, I passed the examination with flying colours and was duly enlisted as a private soldier destined to spend the next several months serving as a batman (officer's servant) to a number of newly appointed lieutenants of about my own age.

This interlude was deliberately contrived by my father, who held it as an article of faith that any officer who had not served time in the ranks would be useless as a leader of fighting men. And he was determined that this was what I was going to become.

My military future brightened when, one autumn day, I was formally presented with the King's Commission—a sheet of imitation parchment formidably inscribed in flowing script:

George the Sixth, by the Grace of God, of Great Britain, Ireland and the British Dominions Beyond the Seas, Defender, Emperor of India, to our Trusty and Well Beloved Farley Mowat, Greetings. We, reposing especial Confidence and Trust in your Loyalty, Courage and Good Conduct, do by

these Presents Constitute and Appoint you to be an Officer of
our Active Militia of our Dominion of Canada in the rank of
Second Lieutenant . . .

The 2nd Battalion of the Hasty Pees, to which I was now posted, was a way station from which I soon expected to be transferred to active service with the 1st Battalion, which had been part of the Canadian Army in England since Christmas, 1939. But neither my efforts nor those of my father seemed able to effect this transfer.

We were stymied by my still-too-youthful guise, as witness this letter to my company commander:

Re: *F.M. Mowat, 2/Lieut, Non-Permanent Active Militia*

1. The further request of the m/n officer for transfer to Active status is herewith noted.
2. It is not considered that the services of this officer with the NPAM should be dispensed with at this time.

(signed)

L.E. Grant, Col.,

H.Q. Military District No. 3.

And scrawled in ink at the bottom of the page:

Sorry, we just can't do it. He looks so damn young there'd be bound to be questions asked in Parliament about the Army baby-snatching!

The militia company to which I was attached consisted of seventy or eighty part-time soldiers—men who were under or over age, had bad medical categories, or were employed in vital war work. Thanks to twenty years of governmental neglect, the militia had no uniforms, modern weapons, or anything much else of a military nature. One had to be inventive, and I was. Out of lengths of sewer pipe I manufactured "3-inch mortars" that fired shells consisting of empty condensed milk cans exploded by giant firecrackers. I also got hold of a photograph of a Bren—the new standard light machine gun, of which there were reputedly six in all of Canada—and had a dozen wooden imitations made in a local furniture factory. These, together with a few score condemned Ross rifles of World War I vintage, provided our armament.

Because I had spent so much of my young life tramping about in the wilds, I was made field craft instructor and as soon as the snow lay deep enough I formed a ski platoon and invented drills and manoeuvres which, since nothing similar had yet been attempted by the regular army, earned me a commendation from District Headquarters, but no transfer.

It was not until the spring of 1941 that I was finally placed on the active list and sent to Fort Frontenac "for disposal," as my orders rather ominously read.

Fort Frontenac belonged to an ancient military past. Behind its limestone walls, grizzled majors and hoary colonels drank whisky from cut-glass decanters in an officers' mess filled with antique silver and faded battle flags. Probationary officers as callow as myself were much impressed by such grandiose and tradition-steeped surroundings. Ceremony was king at Frontenac and I recall how fiercely proud and deeply thrilled I was the day I led a company of properly armed and uniformed regular troops behind the pomp and passion of a military band. *This* was the army of my father's dreams.

Ten days before reaching the magic age of twenty, I was dispatched to an officers' training camp for a qualification course, after which I was sent to Camp Borden, where in the hot summer wastelands of scrubby pines and sand dunes I was introduced for the first time to relatively modern weapons and tactics.

At summer's end my promotion to full lieutenant was confirmed. However, I did not get the immediate overseas posting I had expected. Instead I was seconded to the Borden training staff. Outraged, I had myself paraded before the commanding officer, a resurrected has-been from 1918, and demanded to be allowed to join a draft for England. He was unyielding.

"Not a chance, my lad. You're smart enough to be an instructor but you're not ready to take the gaff with a fighting outfit. *I'll* tell you when you're ready."

I put in a rotten winter, during which my faith in the army began to be clouded by the suspicion that part of it, at any rate, was run by a bunch of stupid old fogies. As a result, I began, in the old army phrase, to swing the lead a bit.

My father, who had his own sources of information, was duly apprised of my altered attitude and in mid-March wrote my mother:

I have to have a fatherly talk with Farley who has been getting somewhat "in the wrong." He does not suffer fools gladly— something which in army life must be done, if not gladly, at least with tact. Once he matures enough to understand that, he should progress rapidly. He has been recommended for a staff course but, though he has made a name in all his courses, I cannot say I want him to get this one. He would eventually go overseas as a staff captain to some higher headquarters but would thus lose the invaluable experience of having led men in action...

I shared my mounting mood of dissatisfaction with other young subalterns, particularly Jerry Austin, who was then my closest friend. As I wrote glumly to my father:

Despondency and dismay fill all of us subalterns. We wonder what the hell was the use of joining up if they're going to keep us here in Canada forever. We've all got bad cases of Bordenitis and swollen mess bills. It's got so bad that last week Jerry and I decided to get rid of our commissions so we could get overseas as privates. Climbing into privates' uniforms we went AWL and hitchhiked to Toronto for the weekend, but the idiots at Headquarters just treated the whole thing as a high-spirited joke! Apparently we can't even *make* them kick us out.

But all things end.

Early in July of 1942 several of us were finally posted for an overseas reinforcement draft, and I hastily scrawled a note to my parents.

Thank heavens, this is it! It's worth two years of waiting. A couple of months' battle training with the Regiment and then, praise be, we'll get a show to try our talents on... Apart from you two, I don't in the least regret leaving Canada even though there is the chance I may not see it again. If we get a damn good lick in at the Hun, it'll be worth it...

On July 18 our troop train pulled out of Borden and forty-eight hours later delivered us to the seaport of Saint John, New Brunswick. Together with several fellow subalterns, I boarded a onetime luxury liner, now become a troop transport, and by midnight we were underway.

ON A GENTLE summer morning we raised the lush, green hills of northern Ireland and at dusk a day later our convoy steamed slowly up the Clyde to dock at Greenoch.

Both banks of the estuary appeared to be sinking beneath a vast proliferation of shipyards whose stocks were filled with the skeletons of new vessels being hastily riveted together to help fill the voids created by the U-boats. The sky was streaked and soiled by gouts of coal smoke rising from the roaring industries associated with the yards. Overhead, barrage balloons tugged at their tethers like blind, bloated beasts striving to escape a sea of suffocating fumes.

There was little time to absorb this fascinating spectacle before we subalterns were bustled into the tiny carriage of a troop train. Engines hooted like demonic owls. The blackout blinds in the carriage were pulled and one meagre yellow bulb illuminated our white and astonishingly childish faces staring at one another in the coal-reek gloom.

Dawn brought us into an immense industrial sprawl where the black cliffs of Blake's "dark satanic mills" were already smearing the pallid sky with dust and smoke. We jolted at a walking pace past endless rows of tenements from whose windows scores of men, women and children leaned out, waving and grinning and shouting raucously: "Good show, Canada!"... "Up the Can-eye-dee-ans!"... "Give the Heinies hell!"

On the last day of July we reached the village of Witley on the edge of the Salisbury Plain well south of London. A herd of double-decked London buses was waiting to trundle us the final few miles to 1st Canadian Infantry Division Reinforcement Unit where Major Stan Ketcheson of the Hasty Pees, a raffish, slightly balding young man, greeted us.

"Glad to see you horny young bastards—though you might better've stayed home. Your regiments don't need you. They're up to their asses in officers, and the only casualties they get are from the syph. So you'll stay here until you're wanted, and we'll teach you something about real soldiering." His sharp-eyed glance flicked from face to face and stopped on mine. "You there, Mowat! How in hell did *you* lie your way into the army? Can't be a day over sixteen, and still a virgin by the look of you. Have to fix that, by God!"

Ketcheson gave us into the charge of one Captain Williams, a worldly older man who began our introduction to England by taking us on a pub crawl through Guildford, the nearest large town, where we quickly learned the vital distinctions between saloon, public and private bars, 'arf-and-'arf and gin-and-it, and between the various women's services.

In the last of several pubs Williams conferred earnestly with a Land Army girl by the name of Phillipa. Shortly thereafter this hefty lady, clad in manure-stained jodhpurs, invited me to take a walk along the adjacent riverbank where, in what must have been the least romantic seduction of modern times, she inveigled me under some dripping bushes and lumpenly stripped me of the virginity I had been vainly trying to shed since the day I joined the army.

"There you are, luv," she said brightly as I fumbled with my fly buttons. "Captain Willy said you needed doing... and there's nothink I wouldn't do for a Canuck!"

I should have been elated but, in truth, I was embarrassed and indignant at the manner in which my long-awaited initiation into Manhood had been arranged. Next day I tried to impress on Captain Williams that if there was any more "doing" to be done, I would prefer to do it myself. Whereat he burst into peals of laughter and thereafter always referred to me as Do-it-yourself Mowat.

Major Ketcheson turned with equal directness to teaching us "real soldiering" by packing us off to a battle drill school where we joined twenty or thirty other raw subalterns in a course that was intended to toughen us up, both physically and psychologically.

It was conducted on a waste of blasted heath overgrown with thorny gorse. Our day began before dawn and lasted until dark, and everything we did, with the exception of defecating, was at the double, weighed down by full battle equipment.

We marched or ran a minimum of ten miles a day and twenty on Sundays. We crawled, squirmed and wriggled for endless hours through gorse thickets while the training staff fired live ammunition under, over and all around us; threw percussion grenades between our outflung legs; or heaved gas canisters (which made us puke) under our noses. For variety we practised unarmed combat with bronzed killers who hit us in the windpipe, kicked us in the testicles, cartwheeled us over their shoulders and belted us across the kidneys with rifle butts.

Although the bayonet was as outmoded in modern warfare as the horse, we nevertheless lined up in front of rows of straw-filled dummy Germans swinging from wooden gibbets, lowered our rifles and thrust our bayonets into the strawmen to an accompanying litany screamed by a hoarse-voiced English sergeant.

"In... Out... Shove it in 'is fucking gut... In... Out... Slit 'is bleeding throat... In... Out... Stick 'im in the balls... In... Out..."

The *pièce de résistance* was a half-mile obstacle course, mostly constructed of barbed wire, that had to be surmounted or crawled under in four minutes flat. One day our personal demon of an instructor decided this was not enough and added a new wrinkle. As we staggered over the last barbed-wire entanglement, he ordered us to double to the right, over a hill, and swim across a pond on the other side.

Somehow we managed the hill and fell rather than ran down the far slope. There was the pond—a huge, open septic tank in which stagnated the sewage from most of the military camps in the Witley area.

The leaders of our panting mob drew up in horror on the edge of this stinking pit, but the demon was right behind us tossing percussion grenades under our tails, so in we plunged...

Before the first week was out we had lost eight or nine of our number, three of them wounded during live firing exercises. The others had been returned to Depot as "unsatisfactory combat material," and I was only a hair's breadth from this fate myself. Nevertheless, I hung on until one morning I awoke to find myself with the symptoms of a dose of clap, a discovery that shocked, disgusted and frightened me.

The camp medical officer made a perfunctory examination, muttered something unkind about people getting what they deserved, and sent me off to collect my kit. I sneaked into the officers' quarters for my gear and sneaked out again like the invisible man. Several ghastly hours later I was admitted to hospital and told that a diagnosis would be made next morning. The nursing sister who showed me to my bed was an attractive woman before whom I felt so shamed I could not look her in the face. I put in one hell of a night. But next morning she flung into my room, threw wide the curtains and brought hope back to a blighted life.

"Well, Lieutenant, lab report is negative. Only a little nonspecific urethritis. Bit like a sinus infection... only not in your nose. Clean it up in a day or three. Meantime, kippers for breakfast? Or would you rather have some nice scrambled powdered eggs?"

Later the senior medical officer inquired, with heavy jocularity, what I had been doing with myself. I refrained from mentioning the incident by the river but I did tell him about the sewage pond, whereupon he grimaced and "guessed" that was where I had picked up the infection. Maybe so, but to this day I find I am uncomfortable in the company of anyone named Phillipa.

Before the day ended I had something else to think about. Both my knees began to swell and soon became so painful I could not stand. I was suffering from bruised cartilages resulting from pounding for too many miles across the heath while laden like a mule. The doctors ruled that I should remain in hospital until I could get about without having to hobble like a geriatric case. This was no great hardship, for the hospital was on the Astor family's Clivedon estate on the banks of the Thames—as lovely a bit of rural England as existed anywhere.

I had walking-out privileges but, since I couldn't walk much, I spent most of three lovely summer weeks of convalescence canoeing on the Thames, watching birds and visiting out-of-the-way pubs. The only fly in the ointment was that most of the other officer patients were considerably senior to me in age and rank and tended to treat me like a boy recruit. Not for the first time I wished I had a thick black beard.

BY THE TIME I got back to Witley most of my erstwhile companions had been posted to their units "in the field," which was something of a blessing for I had returned in mortal dread of the ribbing I could expect because of my "drippy spout." On the other hand, their departure, and the fact that there was no demand for me to join *my* Regiment, left me feeling useless and rejected. I was beginning to believe that perhaps I was too jejune ever to make a proper soldier. My dejection must have showed, for Major Ketcheson went out of his way to bolster my self-esteem.

One of the things he did was to send me on my first visit to London, bearing some very secret documents for Canadian Military Headquarters. Feeling properly important I took the train to Victoria Station where I disembarked into a sea of light-blue, dark-blue and khaki uniforms. Ketcheson had told me to book a room overnight and had suggested I find something close to Trafalgar Square. After some timid inquiries, I fumbled my way to the Underground which eventually disgorged me into the bowels of the earth under the square. Endless flights of escalators carried me to the surface and spewed me out into the blackout, which was intensified that night by a pea-soup fog. When I emerged from the subway station I knew at once what it was like to be struck blind.

Completely adrift I stumbled into gutters, bounced off passersby and fearfully slithered away from the growls of unseen vehicles. I no longer felt in the least like the intrepid messenger indomitably pursuing his vital mission. I felt lost and lonely. At one point I ploughed into the arms of a large, invisible person who must have been an Aussie because he responded with an awesome string of obscenities to my piteous plea for help in finding a hotel. "If I knew where the essing, farking, pussing sots of canting hell these bugging, slicking Limey slucks hid their flagging, mucking hotels, I'd slewing well have me one, mate!" With which he flung me from him and vanished.

Eventually I ran into that bastion of English sanity and safety, a bobby. I recognized him as such because he carried a blue-hooded flashlight in whose unearthly glow I caught a glimpse of many brass buttons.

"Oh, constable!" I cried with heartfelt relief. "Please, can you possibly help me find a hotel?"

Sterling fellows, the London bobbies! This one grunted something unintelligible, gripped my arm with a ham-like hand and propelled me off into the stygian night. Five minutes later he thrust me through a set of blacked-out swinging doors into a brilliantly lit hotel rotunda of unthinkable magnificence. When my eyes had somewhat adjusted to the glitter, I turned to thank him . . . and beheld upon his navy-blue sleeve the one thick and two thin gold stripes of a vice-admiral of the fleet.

"This suit you, Canada?" he asked with a broad grin on his rubicund face. "Best dosshouse in town. Excuse me now. Must jolly well get back on my beat."

MAJOR KETCHESON did other things on my behalf. For one he bestowed a nickname on me. He admired and respected my father, under whom he had served in the peacetime militia, so it was perhaps natural he should tag me with the name my father had borne in the First World War. The name was Squib. Although I at first resented being cast in my father's image in this manner, I soon grew used to the name and even grateful for it when I considered the horrid nicknames I had been cursed with in my school days because of my too-youthful looks, and might all too easily have acquired in the army for the same reason.

Another thing Ketcheson did was find me a batman.

At first glance "Doc" Macdonald seemed unimpressive—a bashful, awkward, apparently ineffectual little fellow of the sort destined to be a victim of the system, whether military or civilian. But within his unprepossessing outer shell there actually dwelt a shrewd and talented survivor. What Doc set out to do or get, Doc did or got—and best to ask no questions if you were the beneficiary of his arcane skills.

Doc and I formed a bond that held throughout the rest of the war years. Most people who saw us together were under the impression it was kindly Farley who had taken Doc under his wing and was looking after him. Only a few close friends ever realized it was the other way about.

SEPTEMBER FINALLY BROUGHT a vacancy for a subaltern with the Hasty Pees. Ketcheson gave me his blessing and next morning Doc and I were on a train bound south and east to join the Regiment, in the field.

The "field" turned out to be the lovely, rolling Sussex countryside in the valley of the River Wal. The companies were billeted in villages, with Battalion Headquarters in a rambling old vicarage in the hamlet of Waldron. When I reported to the adjutant, he had a surprise for me. Instead of being sent to command a rifle platoon as I had expected, I was to begin my service with the unit as intelligence officer.

Although I had only the vaguest idea what an intelligence officer was supposed to be or do, I liked both the sound of the title and the prospect of living at Battalion Headquarters where I would be at the heart of things. My command consisted of a Scout and Sniper Section and an Intelligence Section—some twenty men in all. Fortunately, they were old hands who knew their jobs and so could carry me until I learned the form.

My new job was not all work and no play. There was ample time to explore the countryside, its pubs and villages and, in particular, its birdlife. With the aid of a newly acquired field guide, I was able to tally many species new to me. Eventually my English list included such notables as the bearded tit, chough, hoopoe, twite, chiffchaff, wryneck, dotteral and dabchick. British ornithological nomenclature was anything but dull.

In mid-November the powers that be moved us out of our comfortable billets into a crowded camp consisting of a bleak collection of Nissen huts slowly sinking into a quagmire of sticky mud. As the winter rains began in earnest, these gloomy metal tunnels, from whose corrugations condensation was forever dripping, became increasingly damp and dismal.

To make things worse, the lordly folk at 1st Canadian Corps Headquarters decided the Regiment was due for a turn of the disciplinary screw and afflicted us with a new second-in-command, a hard-mouthed, spear-tongued major with a hyphenated Anglo-Irish name. Major O'Brian-Bennett wasted no time letting us know we had a tiger in our midst. Mud or no mud, rain or no rain, the whole Regiment went back to parade-ground bashing: slogging through close order drill for endless hours in the mindless ritual which is supposed to turn men into soldiers but which all too often turns them into automatons.

Keeping out of O'Brian-Bennett's way became synonymous with survival; but though evasion was possible for the junior officers of the rifle companies, I had to live and work under his cold eye. Clearly he did not approve of what he saw. "Smarten up, Mowat!" and "You'd bloody well better get on the ball!" were amongst his friendlier remarks to me.

On arrival at the unit I had begun to grow a moustache. Although not much to look at—a few pale yellow hairs which could only be seen in a strong light—it was crucial to my self-esteem and I nurtured it in every way I could. One rainy afternoon the new second-in-command turned us all out for a ceremonial inspection. When he got to the Intelligence Section, he halted in front of me and in a voice that could be heard all over the parade square, he shouted:

"Mister Mowat!"

"Sir?"

"What in hell's that on your upper lip?"

"Moustache ... sir."

"Lord Jesus Christ! That's no moustache ... it's a disgrace! A baby could grow a better crop on her pussy! Shave it off!"

Although quaking inwardly I dared not allow myself to be cowed. The entire Regiment was listening and I knew if I did not make a stand I would never live it down. Desperation armed me.

"Sorry... sir. Can't do that... sir. King's Regulations and Orders, section 56, paragraph 8, states that a moustache, once begun, may not be removed without written permission from the commanding officer... sir."

I had him, and he knew it. Lieutenant Colonel Sutcliffe, our commanding officer, was a gentleman and also a gentle man, and he never did give the requisite permission. He was even overheard to remonstrate with the second-in-command for "riding Mowat a bit too hard." O'Brian-Bennett's response did not endear him to me.

"The little pisspot *needs* riding. Take the sass out of him and toughen him up! Lord Jesus Christ, sir, *somebody* has to make a man of him!"

Perhaps this really was his intention toward me but, on the other hand, he may have guessed who had used his own overworked expletive to coin the sobriquet by which he became known within and without the Regiment. Lord Jesus Hyphen Christ.

REAL BATTLE TRAINING had been singularly lacking during my first months with the unit, but in mid-December we were sent north to the Allied Forces Combined Operations Training Centre on Scotland's Loch Fyne. Here we were inducted into the mysteries of making an assault upon an enemy-held coast.

For two exhausting but exhilarating weeks we scurried up and down scramble nets swaying dizzily over icy waters from the sides of troop ships, loading and unloading ourselves from heaving little landing craft. By night, under the lash of winter rain, we practised what we had learned, pitching through heaving seas to stumble ashore in freezing surf on beaches that crackled with simulated machine-gun fire and glared palely under the light of flares.

Since we were convinced this was the prelude to battle, we bore the discomfort uncomplainingly and remained at a high pitch of enthusiasm... until Christmas Day. Shortly after midnight on December 24, we went down the scramble nets into a howling winter's night to make an assault landing on a cliff that, had he faced such an obstacle at Quebec, might have deterred General Wolfe himself. Then, when we had somehow levitated ourselves up this cliff, we were ordered to strike inland across some twenty miles of snowy moors and mountains to capture the "German-held" town of Oban.

It was a night of utter misery and blind confusion. Half-frozen clots of soldiers were scattered about for miles in all directions. In a grey drizzle just before the dawn, I found myself in company with the commanding officer and two signallers, crouching soaked and shivering on a hilltop commanding a distant view of the Loch. The signallers and I were all of his regiment with which Lieutenant Colonel Sutcliffe was still in touch, and the view was the only thing he still commanded. We were listening morosely on a backpack radio for the call signs of some of our missing troops when a message from a powerful base station came booming in.

"Good morning, men!" bellowed an insufferably jolly voice. *"This is the Camp Commandant speaking. I want to wish all troops a most pleasant Christmas. Good show, and carry on!"*

Lieutenant Colonel Sutcliffe snatched the earphones off his head and stared at me with a wild surmise.

"My God, Mowat! Did you hear *that?*"

Before I could reply, one of the signallers interrupted.

"Navy headquarters ship down the Loch is sending an all-station blinker message, sir... *Joyous Yuletide... To all you foot-sloggers... from the... Senior Service...* Shall I acknowledge, sir?"

Sutcliffe seemed to be having trouble finding his voice so I stepped into the breach.

"Yes!" I shrilled, my voice quivering with outrage. "Send: *Shove it up your frigging ass!*"

Slowly Sutcliffe's face relaxed into the beginnings of a smile.

"Well, well," he said mildly. "You might have the makings of a soldier after all..."

A BONE-WEARY REGIMENT returned to Sussex in the first weeks of 1943, yet we were in a good mood, as my journal attests:

Jan. 6. Back in Old Camp Quagmire, which would make one want to vomit except we won't be here long. The assault course training has to mean we'll be going into action soon. Norway seems the most likely bet. We'll never be readier to fight, God knows...

But time slipped by, and nothing happened. Wet, cold and dreary, our spirits sank from day to day as we wallowed in the mindless ritual of barrack life. The real war was becoming increasingly chimerical... something to read about or hear described on the BBC.

The nearest we seemed to get to it was when, in February, Luftwaffe planes began mounting hit-and-run raids on

London. Most were intercepted and forced to jettison their bombs and streak for home. Since our camp lay under one of their favoured routes, we got our share of unexpected presents.

One night hundreds of small incendiaries were dumped over our area. Falling into soft and sodden fields, many of these failed to ignite. Since it was part of my job to know about enemy weapons, I undertook to disassemble one on the cement floor of the Nissen hut I shared with the Roman Catholic chaplain. The padre, a phlegmatic older man, was more or less inured to my eccentricities, but he lost his cool when I accidentally triggered the incendiary and it spouted a white-hot geyser of molten thermite that thrust blinding fingers of flame through the flimsy partition separating his part of the hut from mine.

"Damn your Protestant eyes!" he cried, stumbling through thick smoke toward the door. "It's not *me* that's supposed to roast in hell! It's heathen dolts like *you!*"

Fooling with bombs and other bangers became something of an addiction with me that winter. After four months with my regiment, I was uncomfortably aware that I was still regarded in some quarters more as a mascot than a fighting soldier. Some of my superiors tended to be a shade too kindly, my peers a whit too condescending, and my inferiors a trifle too patronizing. I needed to excel at something martial and reasonably risky and it seemed to me that a flirtation with things that go bang in the night might earn me soldierly merit and the respect of my fellows.

There were a number of Royal Engineer explosive dumps scattered in the fields and woods around us from which I "borrowed" cases of guncotton, slabs of gelignite, boxes of detonators and coils of fuse. I used these in an unofficial demolition course for my scouts and snipers, and we soon became self-taught experts at producing satisfying bangs. But I overreached myself when I decided to see what effect three cases of guncotton would have on a crumbling earthen dam in a nearby training area.

The centre of the dam disintegrated in a great gout of dirt and smoke and the consequent flood roared down a mile-long ditch to inundate the transport park of a British anti-aircraft battery. I departed the scene in haste, but had barely regained the protection of my office when there came a call from Division ordering *me* to investigate the incident. I duly reported that the damage had probably been caused by a bomb jettisoned from a low-flying German aircraft; and thereafter was more circumspect in my adventures with explosives.

THE APPROACH OF spring brought occasional blue skies, and birds began to flock back to England while amorous rabbits bounded and lolloped about on every hand. The season brought a touch of happy madness to most living things but it brought a different kind of insanity to those mysterious beings who governed our lives from the Olympian realms of Army Headquarters. Their reaction to the quickening of the blood was to decree a manic spate of military exercises and schemes which kept us marching and counter-marching across the southern half of England week after dreary week in pursuit of imaginary enemies.

As the weeks drew on, our impatience with the role of uniformed bystanders to a war being fought in other places by other men grew even more intense. We had had a bellyful of training and I was intensely grateful when, in the final days of April, the adjutant informed me I was to be seconded from the unit for detached duty.

"Something called air liaison," he told me. "Haven't a clue what it's all about, but you're to go to a Limey airfield for a month and if you make the grade you may get the chance at a fighting job. Some people have all the bloody luck!"

A pommaded squadron leader at the RAF airfield briefed me on my new employment.

"Air liaison, dear chappy, is the link between you Pongos on the ground and our laddies up in the wild blue yonder. As an air liaison officer, you'll accompany your muddy-footed chums and when they need close support, bombing, strafing, air reconnaissance and all that sort of thing, you'll call on us through your mobile radio link, and we'll oblige. A piece of cake."

Several squadrons were flying operational missions from the field, and for the first time since enlisting I felt I was in touch with real warfare. The atmosphere induced an excitement that kept me going day and night until I felt I had the hang of things. The squadron leader must have thought so too, for at the end of the second week he called me to his office.

"There's a cracking great scheme underway up north," he told me, "and I'm going to pack you off as air liaison officer. You'll have a full squadron of Spits to play about with. *Do* try to keep the Pongos happy, eh? They're *such* a bore when they're upset."

He further explained that I would be wearing two hats. While providing air support and, in particular, air strikes—beat-ups, they were called—for the British "invading force," I would also be expected to do the same for the defenders, and to use my Spitfires impartially to attack either side whenever I found them vulnerable.

So off I went in a comfortable covered truck fitted with several radios manned by two signallers and, for the first time in my military career, discovered I was a somebody. Anxious colonels, brigadiers and even an occasional major-general found their way to my truck to see if I could help their troops out of sticky spots or to beg me to call off my aerial dogs when "enemy" planes were causing them to lose points to the umpires. It was heady stuff for a mere lieutenant.

One lovely, sunny day in mid-May my truck was parked on a commanding hilltop overlooking a winding valley through which ran an arterial road from London. I had not bothered to attend that morning's briefing conference. If they want me, I had reasoned arrogantly, they know where to find me. Consequently, I missed hearing the news that the "front" was to be visited by a Very Important Personage.

My first intimation of anything unusual came when a column of plummy staff cars appeared on the road below, ambling along nose-to-tail in defiance of the strict dispersal rules governing vehicular traffic in front-line areas. I watched incredulously as the column came to a halt in a large, untidy clump at a crossroads. Through my binoculars I could see crisply uniformed staff officers casually descending to wander about with lordly sang-froid while lesser bods began unpacking hampers and setting out food and bottles on folding tables. It was an absolute dream target and within moments I had dispatched a Most Urgent radio message, and had received confirmation that the entire squadron of Spits was scrambling.

The picnickers were just beginning their lunch when out of the south appeared twelve Spitfires in line astern, the thunderous cacophony of their Merlin engines reverberating from the surrounding hills. Down—down—they swooped, and as they roared over the gaggle of cars at three hundred miles an hour and nought feet altitude, red-tabbed officers dived headlong for the ditches with the alacrity of mice fleeing a swooping falcon. I was enthralled by the spectacle, and so was the Spitfire squadron leader. His voice squawked triumphantly out of my loudspeaker:

"Perfectly smashing, chaps! Absolutely top hole! Break starboard now and we'll go round and give it 'em again."

But as the Spits circled wide over the valley to line up for another attack, little puffs of black smoke began to blossom all about them in the clear air. Over the blare of twelve Merlins at full throttle, I heard the unmistakable BOP-BOP-BOP-BOP of Bofors anti-aircraft guns.

"Red leader! Red leader!" The voice over the speaker was suddenly urgent and outraged. *"That's flak! The bloody Pongos've gone crackers! I say, chaps, that's not on! Break port! Break port!"*

At deck level the Spits swung sharply away and in seconds were out of sight. Peace returned to the valley but it held an ominous quality.

Twenty-four hours later I stood stiffly at attention in a wing commander's office. The much-beribboned Winco stared owlishly at me for a time, as if unsure what manner of beast I was. When he finally spoke he sounded bemused.

"Cawn't quite believe it, y'know. No one would, actually. A mere twit of an infantry subaltern... responsible for a full-scale beat-up of Himself? Simply too bloody much!"

The VIP who had come to watch the progress of the scheme, accompanied by the cream of the British general staff, had been no other than the titular commander of us all—His Majesty King George VI.

When the King visited troops in the field, routine orders forbade overflights of any kind in case the Germans might attempt to assassinate him using captured British aircraft. Furthermore, anti-aircraft units were posted about those places where he and his entourage were scheduled to halt, and the gunners were ordered to engage *any* aircraft that came within range.

These were things I had not learned during my freshman weeks as an air liaison officer. I *would* have learned about them if I had attended the morning briefing on that fatal day. I *did* learn about them in the Winco's office, and wondered numbly if this was how a condemned man felt as the judge pronounced sentence of death upon him.

However, the Winco's assessment must have been correct for apparently nobody in authority believed that anything as lowly as myself could have been responsible for such a horrendous blooper. Consequently, my scalp was saved, but nothing could save my future as an air liaison officer.

"You're keen enough, old boy," the pommaded squadron leader explained at my departure. "But we daren't risk keeping you about. Next time you might have a go at Winnie ... Not to worry. After all, who else ever beat up a reigning King of England and lived to tell the tale?"

INSTEAD OF BEING returned to the Regiment, I was ordered to report to the reinforcement camp at Witley. This did not augur well. Gloomily I concluded that, after my contretemps with H.M., the unit would not have me back at any price. However, when I reached the 1st Canadian Division Infantry

Reinforcement Unit, it was to hear the electrifying news that 1st Canadian Division was no longer on the south coast, having moved with great secrecy to Scotland where it was being re-equipped and brought up to full war establishment. There could be no doubt what this presaged—the balloon was finally going up! And I was not to be left out. A week after my arrival at Witley, I was on my way north.

I found the unit billeted in the town of Darvel in Lowland country. It had been lavishly supplied with new jeeps, trucks and armoured carriers, and issued with new weapons. There was a ferment and a feistiness in the air that infected everyone from the commanding officer down. The ambience was so heady I hardly cared when the adjutant rather apologetically told me there was a new intelligence officer—an English captain seconded to us from British Intelligence Corps. I was not even greatly perturbed to find Lord Jesus Hyphen Christ still in his ringmaster's role.

He had me into his office an hour after my arrival "home."

"So, Mowat. Bloody near time you stopped farting about and came back to work! Report to Captain Campbell, OC Able Company. Tell him you're to have Seven Platoon and..." he paused to give me his wolfish grin, "I wish you joy of it."

Alex Campbell was an elephantine lump of a man, red-faced, heavy-browed and fierce-eyed, with an incongruous little Hitlerian moustache. He was possessed of a ferocious determination to kill as many Germans as he could, as they had killed his father in one war and his elder brother in another. The only *good* German, he liked to say, was a dead one—seven days dead under a hot sun. Apart from this fixation, he was a kindly man and, like me, a bit of a poet too.

"Seven Platoon, eh?" he mused after welcoming me into his company. "You must have stepped on the second-in-command's toes good and proper. Seven's the penal platoon, you know. It's where the Regiment's been dumping its hard-case lots, misfits, odds-and-bods, for years. The co's been sending the toughest subalterns he could find to try and tame 'em. Never works... they just maul each other into a ruddy stalemate."

He paused and stared searchingly at me for a moment out of pale-blue eyes, and a ghost of a smile creased his massive face.

"Fancy him sending *you*... a lamb amongst the lions. Well, don't try to face them down. Kind of throw yourself on their mercy, if you take my meaning." He chuckled. "They're a bunch of ruddy carnivores, but they just might make a pet of you... instead of eating you for lunch."

Truth to tell, I was buckling at the knees when I walked out on the parade ground to take over my new command. With a shaking hand I returned the sergeant's sardonic salute and gave the platoon its first order.

"Seven Plato-o-o-n!... ST'NDAT... EASE!"

It was not badly done, except that my voice shot *up* on the pejorative, instead of down.

Sergeant Bates marched them off to a corner of the field where they broke ranks and gathered round to hear my introductory speech.

"Listen, fellows," I began meekly, "the fact is I don't really know too much about a platoon commander's job. But I'm sure as hell willing to learn. I hope you'll bear with me till I do... and give a hand when I need it. Uh, liable to need it quite a lot, I guess. Uh, well, uh, I guess that's about all I've got to say."

It stunned them. They were so used to being challenged to no-holds combat by pugnacious new officers that they did not know what to do with this tail-wagging youngster with his wisp of a moustache, his falsetto tones and his plea for mercy.

I saw rather little of them during the remainder of our stay at Darvel. While the non-commissioned officers kept the men busy, we platoon commanders spent most of our time on refresher courses in combined operations and assault landing. When we weren't doing that, we were wrestling with administrative problems. I spent two entire days locating thirty-one folding bicycles in a distant ordnance depot—and two additional days trying to find the tires that should have come with them.

From the emphasis on assault training, we knew we would be making an opposed landing—but where? A new issue of tropical bush shirts and cotton shorts convinced us for a time that we were destined for Burma. Then we were ordered to repaint our vehicles the colour of desert sand, which seemed to mean we were going to the Middle East. There seemed no end to the number and variety of latrine rumours concerning our ultimate destination, but we did not really care that much. It was enough to know we were finally going into battle.

I wrote to a girl in Canada:

I'm like a kid who's been anticipating a birthday party for years and years and finally sees his mother lighting up the candles. We are about to quit the play-acting and begin living the role we've worked and prepared for so long. I think we'll put up a helluva good show too, though it may take a bit

longer than the propaganda merchants might like to think...
Oddly, I don't feel the least bit scared. Maybe that will come
later, but at the moment I can't wait for the show to open...

It was a time when one made new and bosom friends
almost overnight. One of my fellow platoon commanders in
Able Company was Al Park, a tall, rangy, loose-limbed youth
of my own age. We were billeted together in the same private
house and before a week was out we were as close as brothers.
For a time we shared the services of Doc Macdonald who, during my absence as an air liaison officer, had been working as a
batman-driver in Headquarters Company.

Doc was glad to be back with me. "Jeez, boss, I couldn't
stand that lot. They got no sense of humour there."

This was in reference to Doc's provision of a turkey—a
priceless luxury—to the Headquarters Company officers' mess.
Bad luck led to the discovery that it was really a prize peacock
belonging to a wealthy local laird; but it was rank ingratitude
on the part of Headquarters Company's officers that resulted
in Doc's detention for ten days without pay.

Being reunited with Doc was a great stroke of fortune
but an even greater one was to follow. Lord Jesus Hyphen
came a cropper one morning while riding a motorbike too
fast on a curving road. Some of us had reason to suspect the
bike's brakes had been doctored; in any event, he was carted
off to hospital badly enough injured to be out of circulation
for some time. His replacement was about the last man an
Ontario county regiment could have expected: Major Lord
John Tweedsmuir, a bona fide Lord of the Realm whose father,
onetime Governor General of Canada, was also the famed

adventure novelist, John Buchan. Unlike Lord Hyphen, Lord John was an amiable and sympathetic soul whom we came to cherish and admire.

DURING THE FIRST week of June the unit was granted four days' leave. It was not called embarkation leave, and we were told it was nothing special—which fooled nobody. Men streamed out of Darvel to all points of the British Isles knowing full well that this was their last opportunity to drink in English pubs, make love to English girls and "live, laugh and be merry—for tomorrow we go battle-fighting."

Most of my friends headed south to London, but I thought it foolish to waste half of a too-brief leave riding around on crowded trains. Also it was still springtime and the countryside was calling me. I got out a map of Scotland and did something I had often done as a child—shut my eyes and pricked the map at random with the point of a pencil. Where the pencil landed was where I would go. This time fate selected a region called the Trossachs, only a couple of hours' rail distance from Darvel. I packed my haversack, took my binoculars and bird book and departed.

A meandering local train deposited me at what seemed to be an abandoned station in a valley of misted, glimmering lochs fed by shining tarns that plunged down the slopes of green-mossed mountains. Things all seemed slightly out of focus behind a shimmer of rain as I stood on the empty platform wondering what to do next. There was not even a station master from whom I could inquire about accommodations. As I belted my trench coat and prepared to go in search of shelter, a rattle-trap taxi came snorting toward me. The driver seemed amazed to find that someone had actually descended from the train but when I asked if he could find me a place to stay he nodded me in beside him. Wordless, he drove up an ever-narrowing valley on a gravel road that climbed beyond the last clump of sombre spruce to end in the driveway of an ornate, nineteenth-century castle crouched under the shoulder of a massive sweep of barren hills.

Once the summer seat of a rich marquis, this rococo pile had been closed since the beginning of the war but was now being given a new lease on life as a hotel. However, it was short on guests. Besides myself there were two Canadian and two New Zealand nursing sisters, a Free French naval captain and a young South African armoured corps lieutenant—surely a strangely assorted gaggle of *wander-vögel* to be brought together by whatever chance in this remote cul-de-sac.

The staff, which outnumbered the guests by three to one, consisted mostly of old servitors of the marquis and they displayed an almost pathetic anxiety to make us welcome. The aged butler, now acting as a maître d', pressed on us the finest foods the estate could provide—venison, salmon, grouse, fresh goose eggs, butter, Jersey milk and clotted cream—and pleaded with us to avail ourselves of what remained of the marquis' wine cellar. We slept in regal if slightly musty splendour in vast, echoing apartments, and dined, the handful of us, in a glittering hall beneath chandeliers and candelabra. In the evenings we danced to 1920s music from a wind-up gramophone in the richly panelled trophy room before a mighty fireplace that roared red brands into the moonlit nights.

By day, in a soft veil of warm June rain, or under the watery warmth of a shrouded sun, we climbed among the hills, saw herds of red deer on high, windy ridges; flushed black grouse and capercaillie from the redolent heather of the valleys;

picnicked on venison patties, and drank bitingly cold tarn water mixed with pure malt whisky.

The mood we shared was of time out of time. We were a band of brothers and sisters and so companionable that there was no pairing-off—none of the panting, hectic pursuit of sex that usually dominated the leaves of servicemen and servicewomen. It was a world beyond reality that we so briefly knew together.

But the other world lay waiting. In Greenoch Roads, early in the afternoon of June 13, Able Company of the Hastings and Prince Edward Regiment embarked aboard His Majesty's Transport *Derbyshire*.

PART II

I would have thought of them

—Heedless, within a week of battle—in pity,

Pride in their strength and in the weight and firmness

And link'd beauty of bodies, and pity that

This gay machine of splendour'ld soon be broken,

Thought little of, pashed, scattered . . .

RUPERT BROOKE "FRAGMENT"

MID-AFTERNOON, JULY 1, 1943. The loudspeaker in Troop-deck B crackled as the precise Oxford accent of the ship's adjutant summoned all officers to assemble in the main lounge. I jumped excitedly from my seat beside one of my section corporals on a pile of ammunition boxes.

"It's the tip-off, Hill! Have that quid handy when I get back 'cause this is where you lose a bet!"

Two crowded weeks aboard a troopship bound for an assault landing, without knowing where or when it would take place, except that it would probably be somewhere with a warm climate, had turned us all into betting men. Corporal Hill had bet we'd land in Greece. Everyone else in the platoon had his own opinion, ranging from Istanbul to French West Africa. I had staked my money on Italy—not because I was prescient but because I had earlier overheard one of the divisional staff officers hinting that a knowledge of "Wop lingo" might not come amiss.

I threaded my way through the neat mounds of kitbags and packsacks occupying most of the deck space. As I reached the companionway Doc padded up to me. He wore his usual lopsided grin and was, as usual, unmilitarily familiar.

"While you're with the nobs, boss, pick us up some fags from the officers' canteen, will yuh?" I nodded. It was a losing battle trying to make Doc observe army etiquette. One day, I thought to myself, the colonel's going to hear you talk that way to an officer and he'll have your bloody scalp.

The lounge, which doubled as officers' mess, was already crowded when I arrived. At the forward end a group of staff officers headed by a brigadier was clustered around a huge plaster relief map which had materialized overnight on top of the grand piano. The many small tables scattered about were clotted with officers of every rank and service. I elbowed past a group of British commandos, each sporting a long killing knife at his belt. Beyond them was a coterie of very correct, spiffily dressed officers from the ship's military staff. A clutch of Desert Air Force pilots with silk scarves knotted under stubbled chins and "Thousand Hour Group" hats pushed nonchalantly to the backs of their heads lounged opposite a bunch of Navy sub-lieutenants looking very ill at ease in blue army-style battledress. There were even two flamboyantly attired American liaison officers. But all of these were as the plums and raisins in a pudding composed mainly of khaki-clad officers wearing the insignia of the infantry, artillery, tank, engineer, medical, signals, ordnance and service corps.

Bulking huge as a Titan in that assembly, Alex Campbell, together with Al Park and Paddy Ryan, Able Company's two other platoon commanders, were holding a chair for me. As I crowded in beside them, Al, with a prodigious wink, slipped me a mug of rum and lemon under the table. Alex saw him do it and a frown settled on his heavy face, for he was a vehement temperance man.

The very pukka brigadier, who had been leaning over the plaster map, looked at his watch and held up a hand. The room became dead quiet.

"Now, gentlemen... hrrumph... you will treat what I have to tell you as Most Secret information... is that clear?"

He paused impressively while Al mumbled: "Pompous ass! Does he think there's a Jerry spy with a wireless aboard this tub?"

"The action in which we shall soon be engaged is called Operation Husky. Details will be issued at the Orders Group for unit commanders which will follow immediately. In the meantime, it is my great pleasure to inform you that at dawn, July 10th, you will land on the southwestern tip of Sicily where you will join battle with the enemy in this first dagger-thrust into Fortress Europe."

At the next table an artillery lieutenant slid his bunched fist in front of a companion and let fall a little pile of silver. Someone had guessed wrong.

The brigadier beamed on us like a grandfather who has just presented a long-sought gift to a group of children, then majestically he left the room. The bar reopened and, during the hubbub that followed, I was momentarily alone with my own thoughts. Sicily! I knew next to nothing of the place. Vaguely I recalled something about it being the home of the Mafia, and images of Al Capone and the Saint Valentine's Day massacre came to mind. Then Alex's great hand closed on my arm and squeezed until I winced.

"Not before time, eh, Squib?" he rumbled. "Not before time we sank our teeth into 'em!" There was a savage satisfaction in his voice that gave me pause. He's like a grizzly, I thought: massive and formidable, but harmless enough unless you rouse his ire. I made a mental vow never to give him reason to round on me.

THE FOLLOWING DAYS were frenzied with activity. Orders-groups—O-groups, as they were called—proliferated like chain letters. Colonels were briefed by senior officers from Division, Corps and from Eighth Army, to which famous organization we discovered with a surge of pride we now belonged. The colonels held O-groups for their company commanders, who did the same for their subalterns and we, in turn, briefed our platoons.

Great bundles of pamphlets were broken out of the ship's strongroom and showered upon us. They ranged wildly in subject, from *Handy Italian Phrases* to the order of battle of the German army in Russia. But this was all paper "bumpf" which could be, and mostly was, ignored. What chiefly concerned us was an issue of maps and air photographs of the Pachino Peninsula—the southeastern extremity of Sicily—containing 1st Canadian Division's objective: the town of Pachino and its nearby airfield. We pored over these maps and photos with such avidity that images of them still remain imprinted on my mind.

We platoon officers and our senior non-commissioned officers spent hours studying the plaster relief map in the lounge, painstakingly trying to memorize every hill, hollow, track, hut and clump of olive trees on and inland from Sugar Beach, which was where we were to go ashore.

Throughout daylight hours *Derbyshire*'s decks were as crowded and busy as Waterloo station on Bank Holiday. The weather had grown uncomfortably warm and men sweated through physical training stripped to the waist. Platoons clustered around their officers and listened with unusual and flattering attention to lectures on everything from malaria to German mines. At night the ship murmured with movement as hundreds of men felt their way through blacked-out corridors to the upper decks, practising loading into the assault landing craft which would take them into battle.

Derbyshire was part of a fast convoy consisting of seven big troopers escorted by cruisers, destroyers and corvettes that had zigzagged its way across a thousand miles of ocean to avoid the lurking U-boats off the European coast. At least once a day the escort had hurled salvos of depth charges whose explosions thudded sickeningly against *Derbyshire*'s hull. One evening, just before reaching Gibraltar, they made a kill. Peering through binoculars from an Oerlikon gun platform, Park, Ryan and I watched mighty pillars of water rise against the setting sun like the bloody spoutings of titanic whales. When word was flashed by blinker lamp to tell us the sub was dead, we reacted like kids at a football game. Score one for us! I felt no fear of being torpedoed, had no scorching visions of violent explosions deep in *Derbyshire*'s hull, of flaming pools of oil upon dark waters and men struggling hopelessly therein.

As we entered the narrow throat of the Med we heard the nasal drone of aircraft engines and squinted into the white sky, almost hoping to see the minute midges resolve themselves into Heinkels or Messerschmitts. But the planes high overhead were ours; and through each succeeding day as we steamed into Mussolini's Lake we were overflown by them. "God Bless!" we would greet them as they embossed their invisible patterns in the pale skies.

We passed blacked-out Gibraltar unseen in darkness; but as we stood on deck sniffing the hot land smells, we beheld an astounding spectacle—the Spanish city of Algeciras whose every light was burning as brightly as if the world were still at peace. The sight did not pleasure Alex who was standing near me. I heard him spit angrily over the rail, and grunt:

"Fascist swine! Somebody should put their lights out for good and all!"

By dawn we were well into the Mediterranean. To the south was the golden glimmer of the shores of Spanish Morocco, soon followed by those of Algeria where the Vichy French spun their collaborationist webs.

Hour by hour the tension mounted. All around us the sea and air were pulsing with gathering power as more and more convoys hove into view; new packs of grey destroyers foamed up to guard our flanks; and the planes patrolling overhead multiplied like shrilling locusts.

The convoy command ship became the centre of a maelstrom of activity as tenders and launches (all ships were observing strict radio silence and could communicate only by blinker lamp or messengers) scuttled around her like flotillas of water beetles.

One morning Paddy Ryan stuck his shock of red Irish hair into our tiny cabin and yelled at Park and me to come and "have a dekko." We emerged into the hard sunlight to see the immense bulk of the monitor HMS *Roberts* passing to port. Unbelievably huge, she nevertheless sat so low in the water she was nearly submerged—except for her fighting top and gigantic turrets, each of which tilted its brace of 16-inch guns ominously toward the northern horizon. Her accompanying cruisers and destroyers looked fierce and dangerous enough, but *Roberts* had an aura of brutal power about her that made even the usually unimpressionable Al Park whistle:

"Cor blimey! Wot price yer 'appy 'ome when that big barstard pulls the plug! Wouldn't give two farts in a windstorm for the Jerries on the receiving end!"

The Power and the Glory! It looked as if we would have both upon our side when D-day dawned.

ON JULY 8 I was company orderly officer, and so had to accompany the party of senior officers which daily sniffed its way around the vessel to ensure that everything was properly shipshape. The troops were all up on deck exercising or listening to lectures. As far as I could tell, Able Company's portion of Troopdeck B was in good order; packs neatly stacked, blankets and hammocks rolled, and deal tables scrubbed. Then the staff colonel in charge of the inspection halted abruptly. With his swagger stick he indicated an empty cigarette package lying half-hidden behind a crate of bombs.

"Good God! What's that?" he demanded angrily.

I mumbled an apology and got a withering glance in return.

"Disgusting! See to it at once!"

"Seeing to it" meant routing out the duty orderly who on that day was Private Tiny Sully of my platoon. I could not find him until I tried the heads, which were located directly over the thundering propeller shafts. Peering around in the dim light, gagging on the pervasive latrine stench, I finally spotted Tiny in the farthest corner from the door. For a moment I thought either he or I had gone quite mad.

He was standing at attention with eyes screwed shut, methodically sloping arms and then presenting his rifle for inspection to... nobody. My back hairs prickled as I watched

45

him release the safety catch... pause... slide back the bolt... pause... shove his thumb into the chamber... pause... thrust the barrel forward... pause... then, robot-like, go through the whole procedure in reverse.

The smallest man in the platoon—he was an inch or two shorter than me—Tiny had spent the first sixteen years of his life in an orphanage and had lied his way into the army at seventeen. Although a little withdrawn he had seemed normal enough, but now something had gone badly wrong. His face was the colour of ashes, and rivulets of sweat seemed to be pouring down his cheeks and dribbling off his chin. I took a step or two toward him and was horrified to discover that the sweat was tears—that Sully was weeping uncontrollably.

Having no idea how to handle this situation, I hurried on deck in search of Company Sergeant-Major Nuttley, a slim, dark man in his early thirties who had come to my aid several times since I joined the company. I took him aside and described what I had seen.

"Blue funk, sir, that's all," he told me cheerfully. "Not to worry. I'll soon snap him out of it."

Briskly he turned on his heel but he left me shaken and uneasy. I had never seen anyone give way to fear before, and I could not comprehend how Sully could become like that even *before* the guns began to fire. My God, I thought, if it can happen to him... A jagged sliver of self-doubt slipped between my ribs.

When the bar opened at 1700 hours I was more than ready for it. I joined Paddy Ryan, and we sat together by a big window in leather easy chairs once occupied by first-class passengers, while I drank rum and lemon with determination, trying to put the image of Tiny Sully out of mind.

Paddy was a big, raw-boned maverick whose favourite phrase was "It's a bloody balls-up!" and whose favourite occupation seemed to be puncturing the pomposity of those whom it had pleased the Lord to set in authority over us. On our second day at sea he had won great kudos among us junior officers by posting a cartoon on the orders board at the entrance to the lounge. It showed the rear view of an enormous bull elephant with a tiny mouse looking up in awe at the well-hung giant and saying: *"How true it is! The higher the formation, the bigger the balls!"*

The cartoon was rudely removed moments after the British brigadier who was senior military officer aboard ship caught sight of it, and Paddy had been meditating revenge ever since.

We were on our third or fourth round when the brigadier himself made an entry, accompanied by a covey of staff officers. Paddy at once began to growl like an irate bulldog. "Nattering bastards! No respect for art!" Abruptly he emptied his glass and shoved the table back. "C'mon, Squib! Duty calls!"

Slightly befuddled I followed as he purposefully led the way out of the lounge and down to C Deck where the engineers had stored their assault equipment. Still growling, he unearthed a mine detector, strapped the haversack containing the battery and amplifier on my shoulders, clamped the headphones over my ears, and thrust the mop-like detector unit into my hands. This done, he produced a flask of Navy rum, uncorked it and made me take a shocking big swallow. He had one himself while I struggled to get my breath back.

By now I was both befuddled and bewildered.

"What the hell goes on? Mine detector's no friggin' good on a steel boat, is it? Whatsa game?"

47

"Yours not to question why!" Paddy thrust the bottle at me again. "Up the Irish ivvery toime!"

The lounge was full by the time we returned to it for this was the last night before the dawn of action. The motley crowd was doing its best to drink the bar dry and at first nobody even noticed my odd appearance as we sidled into the room.

I held the detector head in front of me while Paddy walked close behind, his fingers on the volume control of the haversack amplifier.

"Those drinks are ruddy time bombs!" he whispered fiercely in my ear. "Sniff 'em out!"

Obediently I swung the detector over a table crowded with glasses, while Paddy turned up the volume. The resultant high-pitched screeching in the earphones nearly deafened me and was clearly audible to the startled owners of the drinks. Paddy's long arms swept down upon the table and snatched up two glasses—one for each of us.

"Mine lifting detail, gents! Sorry, but these things is lethal."

Standing by the bar the brigadier watched our progress from table to table with what was clearly a jaundiced eye. But although his bushy moustache twitched with irritation, he was not about to demean himself by taking overt notice of our antics. As we worked our way closer to him he deliberately turned his back and began talking to a red-tabbed major of his staff. All eyes were on us now and the hubbub was dying away as Paddy muttered a peremptory order: "Check his bum!"

Obediently I raised the detector head and, as it came level with those well-pressed serge trousers, Paddy turned the amplifier up as far as it would go.

The subsequent squeal could be heard all over the now utterly silent room. The brigadier twitched convulsively, but he was made of solid stuff. He did not turn ... not, that is, until Paddy leaned over me, tapped him on the shoulder and proclaimed in a concerned and ringing voice:

"Begging your pardon, sir. Looks like you got a booby trap shoved up your ass!"

In the pandemonium that followed I vaguely remember being held up on my feet by a magenta-faced Alex Campbell while Lieutenant Colonel George Renison, the senior Canadian aboard ship, addressed himself to me.

"You lucky little twerp! You'll never know how close to a court martial you two've just come! If it hadn't been that we'll be in action in thirty-six hours..." He turned his head away, unable to contain his laughter.

It was a great evening. One to cherish in the days ahead.

WHEN I BLEARILY opened my eyes next morning it was to discover we were under attack—not by any human antagonist but by the sirocco. Born in the furnace of the Sahara, this baleful wind had come roaring northward over the Mediterranean in the early hours before dawn, seemingly intent on scattering the vast flotilla of big and little ships which was even then turning north toward Sicily.

Derbyshire was wallowing like a drunken sow. All the loose gear in our cabin had been pitched to the floor where it slithered and clattered back and forth as the ship lurched and rolled. For the first time since we had been together, Doc was not on hand to get me started on my day. When I struggled down into the noisome fug of the troop decks, I understood the reason for his absence. Troopdeck B was a shambles. Many of the men still swung in their hammocks, green and groaning and unable or unwilling even to sit up. The smell of puke and engine oil was overwhelming. Everything that was not lashed down had come adrift: kitbags, weapons boxes, steel crates of ammunition, mess tins, tin helmets and nameless flotsam surged back and forth among the upturned tables, banging into stanchions and fetching up at the end of each long roll in dishevelled heaps against the bulkheads. The din was deafening but by virtue of screaming myself hoarse I managed to get most of the seasick men headed up the companionway to the main deck where they would at least be able to breathe.

Platoon Sergeant Bates and a few others, who, like me, were relatively immune to seasickness, pitched in to try and bring some order out of chaos. It was exciting work. A box of Mills grenades had broken open and the deadly little bombs were hurtling back and forth like so many hard-pitched baseballs. Bates was hit in the back of the legs by a charging crate of ammo and sent slithering down the canted, greasy deck. As I helped him to his feet his temper flared:

"Fuckingsonofawhore! Worse than a goddamn rodeo!"

There were few customers in the officers' dining room when I swayed my way up to it in search of breakfast. Alex had made it, though barely, and his usually ruddy face was the colour of Gruyère cheese. He averted his eyes as a steward skated up and slapped a plate of boiled kippers in front of me.

"Sheer sadism!" he groaned. "Only the Limeys would play a rotten trick like that on a dying man ... and, Squib, I'm dying certainly." He slumped in his chair like a hung-over walrus, but even in the queasy grip of seasickness his presence still dominated the heaving room.

Beyond the ship the scene was something to behold. The sky was as harshly bright and clear as ever, for the sirocco brought no clouds in its train. The sun streamed down upon a waste of heaving seas, foaming white to the horizon. And the great invasion fleet—that irresistible weapon—was in total and almost helpless disarray. The largest warships were being swept by breaking seas until they looked like half-awash submarines. The big troopers were being staggered by the impact of the greybeards that broke over their heaving sterns. Most of the smaller vessels had turned about and were hove-to, head to the sea and wind, and some of them—particularly the square-nosed tank landing craft—were obviously nearing the limits of their endurance. If the gale had increased in strength only a little more, many of those metal boxes would have swamped and sunk. I thanked my stars I wasn't aboard one of them . . . and then remembered that in less than twenty-four hours we were due to be cast into that turmoil of white waters in tiny assault boats which were little more than sardine cans and not much more seaworthy.

In mid-morning a blinker message flashed from the convoy command ship. Shortly thereafter we were told that, unless the weather had moderated by tea time, Operation Husky would be postponed. Those suffering the worst agonies of seasickness could hardly have cared less, but the rest of us were filled with gloomy forebodings. So far as we knew, our presence, or at least our intentions, remained unknown to the enemy. Surprise—that vital element of any invasion—presumably remained with us. But if we had to spend an entire day hovering off the coasts of Sicily, the enemy would be bound to discover us and to deduce where our thrust would be directed, and then we would become a dream target for German and Italian aircraft, subs and even motor torpedo boats.

"They'll have to cancel the ruddy thing," Alex grumbled furiously. "And then God only knows when we'll get another chance to stick it to the Hun!"

However, shortly after 1600 hours the wind started to fall and by 1700 had practically dropped out. The great seas began to subside and at 2000 hours Park and I were called from admiration of a flaming sunset to be told that "the show was on."

We three subalterns, together with our platoon sergeants and Company Sergeant-Major Nuttley, wedged ourselves into Alex's tiny cabin while for the last time he went over the orders for the assault. Muted music from the BBC was playing on the public address system and with a start I recognized the repetitive strains of Ravel's *Bolero*. I had not heard it since an evening in Richmond Hill shortly before sailing for England when, alone in an empty house, I had played the record over and over again to help assuage the misery of having been rejected by a girl with whom I thought I was totally in love. Her image came back to memory now, and I realized with faint surprise that I no longer gave a damn about her. I was wondering if I ever really had ... when the music was abruptly stilled and the voice of the ship's adjutant came booming in upon us.

"Do you hear there? Do you hear there? Serial leaders join your serials now ... I say again ... Serial leaders join your serials now ..."

WHEN I REACHED the troopdeck I found most of my crowd lounging on wooden benches around the mess tables watching Corporal Mitchuk of No. 2 Section and some of his special cronies playing blackjack. A naked light bulb swaying over the table threw Mitchuk's Slavic features into sullen relief. He looked what he was: a heavy-handed fighter who never knew when to quit. Next to him sat Ernie Thompson, number-one man on the platoon's 2-inch mortar. Ernie, who was reputed to have been a Golden Gloves contender, had once spent sixty days in the Glasshouse—the dreaded British military prison— for knocking an officer unconscious during a pub brawl. I tended to treat him with somewhat exaggerated respect.

Looking and acting tough was *de rigueur* for most of the men of Seven Platoon, but not all were roughnecks. Sitting beside the card players because the light was better there, yet totally detached from them, Private A.K. Long was immersed in a limp, leather-bound volume of Shelley's poetry.

A.K. was a conundrum. His elder brother was an officer in Dog Company and A.K. could have been one too, for he had all the right connections, but for reasons none of us could fathom he had chosen to remain a ranker who would not even accept a lance-corporal's single stripe. He was the one man in the platoon I might have felt at ease with, but he remained as pleasantly aloof from me as from the rest of the platoon. Oddly, he was not resented, perhaps because of his almost feline air of intractable independence. It was this independent attitude which had led to his being banished to Seven Platoon; for although he was never impolite and was unfailingly gentle in his manner, if he did not choose to obey an order nothing in God's earth could force him to it.

For a time I stood in the shifting shadows near a bulk-head—the ship was still rolling heavily—my presence ignored by everyone. I felt a need for reassurance and I looked toward two stocky, round-faced youngsters who sat together at the end of one of the tables. Sharon and Robinson might have been brothers, but were not. Two farm boys, they were the very stuff of which the Regiment was made, and from which it took the name by which it was known throughout the division—the Plough Jockeys. These two sat in easy and companionable silence, smoking slowly and thinking their own placid thoughts. I felt a wave of affection for them and wondered what witless military decision had doomed them to the Penal Platoon.

The *click-snap* of a rifle bolt being worked made me turn sharply. Tiny Sully was sitting on some crates in a dark cul-de-sac behind the companion stairs. Dim as the light was, I could see that he was holding his rifle with the muzzle resting on the toe of his right boot while he mechanically shoved the bolt home, pressed the trigger on an empty chamber, recocked the weapon and pressed the trigger yet again. In three strides I was beside him, hissing into his ear with a savagery I had not known I was capable of.

"Put that rifle down, you crazy little bastard! You shoot your toe off now and Mitchuk'll put a bullet through your head! You don't get off that easy."

My hands were slimed with sweat and my legs were shaking as I turned away from him. I felt unutterably alone now—no part of this group of men in bush shirts and shorts sitting stolidly in the steaming fug of the mess deck waiting with apparent unconcern for the impersonal voice of the dispatcher to call our number—serial sixty-seven—over the loudspeaker.

"Do you hear there? Do you hear there? Attention serial seventeen. To your boat station move... Serial eighteen, stand by..."

In neighbouring Nine Platoon's area someone was strumming on a Jew's harp and a seaman was moving through the murk distributing cans of self-heating soup and bandying insults with the Pongos—derogatory Royal naval slang for soldiers—in a flat, cockney whine. Gratefully I saw Al Park beckoning to me. As I made my way toward him, I thought how out of place he looked in our grimly military assemblage. Gawky, loose-limbed as a stork, his stovepipe shorts and flapping bush shirt gave him the appearance of a cartoon Boy Scout. But if he realized how odd he looked, it did not bother him. Nothing much seemed to bother Al whose sense of the ridiculous foreshadowed the advent of Woody Allen. Together we stumbled and slid through the cramped company area, checking the gear and kit for the umpteenth time without really being aware of what we were doing.

Something skittered away underfoot and Al thought it was a mouse. For a few minutes we were diverted as I reminded him of the Intelligent Mouse which had shared quarters with us at Darvel and had become so familiar that, one Saturday night, it crawled into a nearly empty mug of rum and got itself besotted. Al put it tenderly to bed in a cardboard box full of Alex Campbell's khaki ties, and we forgot about it until next morning when Alex started fumbling for a tie to wear on Church Parade...

"... *Attention serial forty-five. To your boat station move...*"

"Getting closer," Al muttered. "Best get back to my brood."

Alone again I looked at my watch: 0015 hours. I wondered what was happening outside the ship. My thoughts hovered uneasily over the plaster map model. Were the enemy gunners sleeping in the machine-gun post on the point of land called

Grotticello, which dominated our beach? Or were they gazing tensely across the phosphorescent shimmer of the heaving sea toward an alien shadow in the south? Was one of them even now ringing the field telephone that linked him with his headquarters? Perhaps the call had already been made! Perhaps the engines of Savoia-Marchettis and Junkers 88s were already roaring into life on Pachino airfield... My bowels began to constrict...

"...Do you hear there? Attention serial fifty-two..."

There was a stir at the far end of Troopdeck B as men of the 48th Highlanders began scrambling to their feet, adjusting their web equipment, picking up their rifles, Sten guns, mortars and Brens. An officer's voice, high-pitched and querulous, cut through the murk. Ernie Thompson looked up from his cards and casually acknowledged my presence.

"How much time we got, Skipper?"

"Ten minutes maybe," I replied in a voice marshmallowy with gratitude. *He had called me Skipper!*

He grunted and dropped another shilling in the pot. The game went on...

"...Serial sixty-seven... Serial sixty-seven, stand by..." Mitchuk flung his hand over his shoulder. "Fuck this," he shouted as the cards fluttered to the greasy deck. "I fold!"

One or two men laughed in a brief, constrained way and then they were all on their feet, groping for their gear, shoving into position.

"...Serial sixty-seven. To your boat station move..."

The platoon lined up in single file. Doc's fingers were hooked into my web belt and the rest of the men following behind were linked to him in the same manner. Platoon linked to platoon until the company coiled in and out behind me like a great serpent.

Alex appeared alongside. "All right, Squib. Let's get going!"

We shuffled up the companion stairs and into the thick darkness of a corridor. A blue-hooded flashlight shone briefly on another column converging from a side passage to join the slow stream flowing toward the upper decks. The men were faceless and indistinct, like figures in some sombre dream. The light went out and I thrust a hand ahead of me as if to cleave my way through a darkness that was palpable. There was no sound except the hissing of heavy breathing and the gritty slither of iron-shod boots on steel plating.

Suddenly fresh air was riffling over my sweaty face. A door opening framed a starlit sky that was so brilliant compared to the stygian gloom from which we were emerging that it seemed dazzling. We moved more rapidly along the open deck to our designated landing craft which was swaying in its davits like a monstrous, ugly cradle dangling between wind and water.

I stood aside as the men began clambering over the rails, staggering under the battle gear that weighed them down like beasts of burden. When the last had fumbled his way to a place on one of three long benches running the length of the craft, I realized I had not seen Tiny Sully.

"Where's Sully?" I demanded urgently.

Someone in the dark belly of the landing craft made a lugubrious, gasping sound and once again I felt my bowels constrict. Then came Sergeant Bates's contemptuous voice:

"He's here, the little shit!"

I had barely reached my place in the bow when the night was shattered by an infernal clamour as all the winches on

Derbyshire's deck began to clatter in unison and thirty landing craft descended toward the sea below.

We hit the water with a resounding splash, then lurched violently against the mother ship with a clangour of steel on steel that made me cringe in fearful certainty that the sound would be heard in Pachino itself. Our Royal Navy coxswain, holed-up in a tiny armoured cubbyhole on the starboard bow, cursed viciously, swung the helm hard over and rammed down the throttle. Someone cast off the falls and we swung bucking and jolting into the muttering darkness.

There were perhaps four hundred vessels of every size and shape gathered at our rendezvous some seven miles off the coast of Sicily, and the muted putter of their engines blended into one pervasive rumble as if of some uneasy giant in restless sleep.

Standing in the bows beside the coxswain's cubbyhole I could just manage to peer over the high gunwales. The night was full of looming shadows, and the heaving waters were patterned with the glimmering phosphorescent wash of unseen boats. A sudden lurch caught me off balance and I stumbled back into the lap of Corporal Hill who, as if this had been some awaited signal, was immediately sick all over my back and shoulders. His example was infectious and men were soon retching their hearts out from one end of the boat to the other. I clawed my way back to the rail and fought my own rising nausea by staring fixedly at a pinpoint of green light on the stern of some unseen craft ahead of us.

Rupert Brooke's "A Channel Passage" came unbidden into mind and I remembered his remedy for seasickness—think hard of the girl you love: *Now there's a choice—a sea-sick body, or a you-sick soul!*

"You fucking cow!"

The cox swore stridently as the boat breasted a heavy sea and fell off sideways into the trough.

"You she-bitch female fucker!"... whereupon he too was sick.

The interior of the boat was becoming something of a shambles.

As she pitched and yawed, the mass of men slid helplessly up and down the benches, their feet in a broth of their own vomit. Some were pleading with me to let them go to the gunwales; but I dared not even let them stand, for assault landing craft were notoriously unstable in rough water and could easily turn turtle if the weight shifted from one side to the other. To my surprise I found myself taking real command of my platoon for the first time.

"Don't anyone bloody well move," I shouted over the guttural roar of the diesel engine, "or we'll all be in the drink, and it's too damn far to swim!"

Nobody made a move to disobey me, perhaps because they were too sick; and I was feeling rather marvellous until the cox reached out of his cubby, caught my arm and pulled me close.

"We're fucking well lost, ducky! Can't find no bleedin' marker buoy! Wot yer wanter do?"

He had been searching for a floating marker that bore coded lights—blue over white over blue—the rendezvous point from which we were to steer a compass course to our designated beach. Without that fixed departure point we were lost indeed. And since *my* boat led the company, *mine* was the responsibility.

Panic engulfed me. There was nobody I could call on for help. In the first glow of the false dawn I could just make out the box-like shapes of the other two craft dimly visible astern. I glanced at my watch and saw that zero hour was only minutes away. There was no time, nor was this heaving ocean the place for a conference!

Frantic, I tried to guess where we might be. Dead reckoning might have given a real sailor some clue but I had never been more than a playtime sailor. The eastern horizon was rapidly lightening. The balloon would be going up any moment now! I swallowed hard, and in a voice that shrilled like a tin whistle gave the cox an order.

"Steer 340 degrees!"

It was the proper course (indelibly fixed in my memory) but *only* if followed from the correct departure point.

Obediently the little vessel swung off and headed for the unseen land. Moments later a necklace of bright-red jewels floated eerily into the northern sky off our starboard bow. The first enemy gun had opened fire! From the stern I heard Bates bawl: "There goes the ball game, boys!"

Idiotically I bellowed back: "Take cover, men!"

Then the waning night was ripped asunder by such an eruption of sound and fury as might have marked the world's beginning... or its end.

HMS *Roberts* had triggered the opening of the naval barrage with a full broadside. Four incandescent spheres burst from her suddenly revealed grey bulk—four suns, rising with the speed of thought, that seemed to ignite the whole arc of the southern horizon in flickering red and yellow lightning as squadron after squadron of warships opened fire. It took perhaps three seconds for the sound to hit us and then we were cowering below the gunwales, hands over ears, as cataclysmic thunder overwhelmed our world.

I saw the cox beckoning urgently. Even with his mouth hard against my ear I could barely hear him shout.

"Yer want me to tike 'er in? Too bleedin' 'ot out 'ere!"

Dawn was breaking and a low, pale shoreline was emerging into view a mile ahead of us. So close to it that they seemed to be on the yellow beaches, a pair of shoal-draft support craft were racing along laying a billowing smoke screen to hide us from the enemy. I scanned that formless strip of land with agonized intensity, desperately hoping to recognize some landmark. Nothing looked familiar, but there seemed to be a spit of land off to our right and I prayed it might be the one which marked the Regiment's left boundary.

"Steer to the right of that point!" I screamed to the cox just as a salvo of *Roberts'* 16-inch shells passed directly overhead like a hundred express trains roaring through some titanic tunnel.

The cox nodded grimly and opened the throttle. The boat reared back, digging her stern into the swells. A glance astern showed our two sister vessels following in arrowhead formation. I could see Alex standing in the bows of the starboard one, bull head thrust forward under his ridiculously small steel helmet. He was cradling a Bren and firing brief bursts toward the shore. As if in answer, streams of tracer began to arch toward us from a red-roofed building on a knoll a few hundred yards inland from the beach. I ducked as tiny spurts of water stitched between Alex's boat and mine. Hunched against the landing ramp I waited, revolver clenched in sweating palm, for the grinding moment when we would hit the beach.

A vast, yeasty waterspout appeared alongside and seemed to hang suspended over us. There was a brutal, juddering thump, then we were drenched in warm salt water that smelled and tasted of brimstone. I jumped so violently that I mashed my knuckles on the ramp. First blood, I thought foolishly.

Then we touched down—but not upon the beach. Instead, we struck an uncharted sandbar lying a hundred yards offshore. And we hit it only seconds before a salvo of 6-inch shells from one of the cruisers whomped into the beach directly in front of us. *Wumpety-wump-wump-wump,* they roared. Shell fragments whanged against the boat while Seven Platoon and its intrepid leader sprawled on their collective belly. Had that shoal *not* existed we would have been obliterated by the salvo from our own guns—and probably no one would ever have been the wiser. Nevertheless, the bar was not an unmitigated blessing.

The cox let the bow ramp down with a rattling run and fairly shrieked at us to get off his boat. He was in one hell of a hurry to get out of there, and as I realized how desperately naked we were in our tin can now standing wide open to the enemy... so was I!

This was the moment toward which all my years of army training had been building. It was *my* moment—and if I seized it with somewhat palsied hands, at least I did my best.

Revolver in hand, Tommy gun slung over my shoulder, web equipment bulging with grenades and ammo, tin hat pulled firmly down around my ears, I sprinted to the edge of the ramp shouting, "Follow me, men!"... and leapt off into eight feet of water.

Weighted as I was I went down like a stone, striking the bottom feet-first. So astounded was I by this unexpected descent into the depths that I made no attempt to thrash my way back to the surface. I simply walked straight on until my head emerged. Then I turned with some faint thought of shouting a warning to my men, and was in time to see Sergeant-Major Nuttley go off the end of the ramp with rifle held at arm's length and the fingers of his free hand firmly clutching his nose. He looked like an oddly outfitted little boy jumping into the old swimming hole.

The other two landing craft were in the same pass as ourselves but I noted with a thrill of pride that I seemed to be the first to have reached shore. I stumbled on through the shallows until I saw little spurts of sand racing down the beach in my direction. Automatically I dropped on my belly and a big roller picked me up and carried me, helpless to resist, toward the stitching machine-gun bullets, dropping me just short of that deadly pattern.

The day was warming fast as the red sun swelled over a windless horizon. The sand gleamed golden and serene and I smelled the perfume of strange flowers. I rolled over and looked seaward and saw a hundred men wallowing comically out of the depths, like a herd of seals hurrying to land upon a mating beach. Two of the landing craft had already backed off the bar and were hightailing it away. Our own was still immobile, and in a moment I saw why.

She was empty except for her crew... and one small khaki figure standing stiffly at attention in the gaping bow opening. Suddenly he began to move, *marching* up the ramp, rifle at the slope, free arm swinging level with his shoulders. Tiny Sully was coming off that sardine can as if on ceremonial parade at Aldershot... except that his eyes were screwed tight shut.

A cluster of mortar bombs shrilled out of the pellucid sky, and the waters into which Tiny had plunged boiled upward with visceral thunder. Tiny Sully had gone from us... marching blindly to Valhalla.

The naval barrage had moved inland by now and things were a little quieter—quiet enough so I could hear the wicked spatter of small arms fire coming at us from the cluster of farm buildings overlooking the beach. Most of my platoon had now joined me, lying half in and half out of the surf. This was clearly no place to linger, but the way ahead was barred by a thicket of barbed wire which undoubtedly was mined.

Sergeant-Major Nuttley flopped down beside me, yelling: "Somebody blow that wire! Where the hell's the bangalores?"

I turned my head, looking for inspiration, and saw Alex come charging ashore like an enraged monster rising from primeval seas. He bellowed something and pounded past me to slide a bangalore torpedo—a ten-foot length of pipe stuffed with explosive—under the wire. It went off with a smashing crack, then we were on our feet following Alex through the gap, our heavy boots sinking and slipping in the soft and shifting sand.

I did not notice, but Sergeant-Major Nuttley was not with us. He remained lying at the water's edge... dead, with a bullet through his throat. He had been lying within arm's reach of me, and yet I did not know.

Beyond the beach we entered a rustling maze of canebrakes growing between high dunes. Here we milled aimlessly about like a mob of overburdened donkeys until Alex loomed over us and began giving orders for an attack on the enemy-held buildings.

He issued his orders in the formal manner prescribed in the military textbooks, but these seemed incomprehensible, even senseless. We stood about looking puzzled until Alex began to wave his arms and bellow at us. Then I saw that blood was gushing from his right arm in a spout of impressive size. I rushed over and caught the wounded arm as it flailed over his head. Only then did Alex realize he had been hit. A bullet had gone cleanly through the muscle of his upper arm, and in the excitement of the moment he had felt nothing.

He subsided with a look of fatuous surprise on his great, moon face, while a stretcher-bearer applied a shell dressing and staunched the flow of blood. Then Alex gave us the first of the new kind of orders which were to become routine in the days ahead.

"What're you waiting for? Get up to that ruddy house and knock those buggers out!"

Since he seemed to be speaking directly to me, I rushed off through the canes, my men stumbling on my heels. We emerged in a parched little field below a low hill with a cluster of stone buildings on its summit. Ernie Thompson, number one mortar man, dropped into a drainage ditch, unlimbered his weapon and without orders fired off all his smoke bombs. The rest of us plunged on until we fetched up like a bunch of driven rabbits against another barbed wire obstacle.

I don't know what the enemy was doing all this time—presumably shooting at us—but he must have been unnerved by our unorthodox behaviour since none of us was hit. We lay there in front of the wire, completely exposed but with every weapon in the platoon blasting away full tilt. In three or four minutes we had nearly exhausted our ammunition and would shortly have been reduced to throwing rocks had not a most unexpected thing occurred.

From somewhere ahead of us a voice screamed: *"Hold your fire, you clods!"*

Such was our astonishment that we immediately obeyed, never pausing to consider whether or not this might be an enemy ruse. Action was called for, and it was up to me to do the calling.

"Fix bayonets!" I shrilled.

And so we went into our first and last bayonet charge in a war in which the bayonet was an almost total anachronism.

We scrambled over the wire, ripping our shorts and shirts and flesh, and went galloping clumsily up the slope. As we reached the crest we discovered why we had not all been slaughtered during this suicidal attack. A group of commandos was just completing an assault from the rear of the hill: only, instead of waving bayonets, they were sensibly hosing streams of lead into the buildings.

"Cor!" a commando sergeant said to me after we had finished sorting ourselves out. "You chaps *did* look loverly! Just like the Light Brigade. Never seen nothin' like it 'cept in that flick with Errol Flynn!"

For a second I was taken in—until I noticed the sardonic grins on the faces of his men.

The surviving Italian defenders of the farm were herded out into the morning's brilliant glare, hands locked behind their heads and looking as harmless as a Salvation Army soup-kitchen line. There was some argument about ownership of them, which Alex settled when he arrived on the scene, puffing heavily, his big face a dusky magenta, and his wounded arm thrust, Napoleon-like, into his bush shirt. "Let the Limeys have them!" he thundered at us. "Why aren't you pushing on?"

"Push on where?" I asked him. "I don't even know where we're *at!*"

The commando lieutenant was able to put us right about that, and so we discovered that, under my pilotage, Able Company had made its own assault on Sicily—several miles to the westward of where we were supposed to land, and well beyond the outer edge of Eighth Army's beachhead. We and the commando squad—which had been detailed to knock out a non-existent coastal battery—were now all alone away out in left field.

A PRUDENT COMPANY commander would now have turned eastward into the beachhead in search of his battalion, but Alex was not feeling prudent. He chose, instead, to strike due north into the interior of Sicily.

"Go for their guts before they get their guard up!" he told us fiercely. "Knock 'em on the head before they're out of bed!"

He got no argument from us, for we were like overtrained gun dogs just released into a cloud of powder smoke, and dead keen to go. The apprehension which had knifed into my guts before we left *Derbyshire* had vanished in the heat of action. Although I had just seen the first of my comrades die, I had not yet seen the face of death, and so was fearless still.

We marched out of the farmyard in textbook battle order, single file by sections, with three-yard intervals between men. The farm track soon brought us to a narrow dirt road meandering northward over a sun-baked coastal plain between cactus hedges aflame with yellow flowers. These garish blossoms together with the red-tiled roofs of the scattered stone farm buildings provided the only splashes of colour in an otherwise achromatic landscape. As the sun climbed higher, even the blue sky blanched to hueless pewter. Parched grapevines and stunted grain crops in a patchwork of minuscule fields along our way showed only the faintest wash of green through layers of floury dust. The whole countryside seemed to be an incipient desert and no living creature was anywhere visible except for an occasional high-soaring vulture, sharp-eyed for carrion. People and farm animals which might have been expected to inhabit this arid land were nowhere to be seen. As we halted by the roadside for a few minutes' rest, I drew Al Park's attention to the absence of humanity.

He grinned. "No mystery, Squib. They've all buggered off to the good ole U.S. of A. And you sure as hell can't blame 'em!"

Alex came lumbering up, his face flaming in the heat.

"Mowat! Get off your butt! Take a patrol to that bunch of buildings over there. Something's moving."

Corporal Hill and his section joined me and cautiously we made our way across some desiccated vineyards into a field which was, incredibly, covered with huge, ripe watermelons. I heard a *thuck* and turned to see A.K. Long's face disappearing into a dripping chunk of melon.

"For Christ's sake!" I hissed. "You think you're at a fair? Drop that bloody thing!"

"No harm, sir," Long replied gently. "Here, have a slice yourself."

The temptation was irresistible. With a guilty glance to assure myself that Alex and the rest of the company could not see us, I joined my men who were now squatting like schoolboys in the middle of the melon patch. Somebody handed me a piece and I was just taking my first juicy bite when a raucous voice bellowed:

"Yew ovah theah! Which side yew on?"

From behind the shelter of a low stone wall at the edge of the melon field, three strapping big men wearing camouflage

68

uniforms had materialized, and they were covering us with automatic rifles. For one awful moment I took them to be German paratroopers, then I recognized the insignia on their shoulder patches.

"Canadians! We're on your side!" I bawled.

"Goddamn good thing, buddy. Else yew all be daid shit-heads by now!"

They were survivors of a U.S. airborne division which was to have landed fifty miles to the westward of our beaches. But having been dropped with haphazard abandon during the night, the luckier parachutists had been strewn like confetti across much of southern Sicily, while scores of their unluckier comrades had landed in the sea.

Before we parted—we to rejoin our company and they to make their way down to the beach, which we assured them was now in Allied hands—I made an exchange with one of them: my .38 Smith and Wesson revolver (about as useful in modern warfare as an arquebus) for his .30-calibre semi-automatic carbine. This weapon was something the like of which none of us had ever seen before, and its possession subsequently made me an object of much envy. On one occasion the batman of the lieutenant colonel commanding the Royal Canadian Regiment stole it from me for his boss. But he reckoned without Doc, who not only tracked the weapon down and got it back but also extracted a priceless bottle of Haig and Haig from the RCR as hush money.

Alex was not pleased when I reported back to him.

"First it's Limey commandos," he complained. "Now it's flaming Yanks! Next it'll be the Mounties' Musical Ride! Where the devil's the *en*emy?"

Able Company set out to see if it could find him some.

With Paddy Ryan and his platoon leading, we marched steadily inland, apparently alone in an abandoned world. It was a most peculiar sensation. The guns behind us had mostly gone silent and there was no indication that war had a place in these empty fields which lay shimmering and unreal beneath the sun's blinding glare. Ahead of us the baking plains wrinkled upward into eroded hills that lifted to distant ranges of what might have been lunar mountains. It was as if we were a troop of actors who, having played our role upon the beaches, were now marching off stage into an enormous limbo.

The heat, the silence and the aftermath of a sleepless night and battle in the dawn began to take effect. I was drowsing on my feet when there came a low rumble from up ahead, followed by a sharp rattle of rifle fire and the heavy coughing of a Tommy gun.

Rounding a bend in the road, the men of Paddy Ryan's platoon had virtually collided with an enemy artillery troop bound south toward the beaches.

By the time I reached the scene, a dozen Italian soldiers in ill-fitting greenish uniforms stood huddled in the middle of the road, their hands held high. Two wooden-wheeled field guns—antiquated relics of the First War—were slewed into the ditches where they had been dragged by their teams of terrified horses. Beyond the guns an ancient truck blocked the narrow road, its radiator geysering a plume of steam. It might have been a rather comic spectacle... except that on the dusty verge lay three inert human forms.

Paddy was down on one bare knee beside them, feeling gingerly for signs of life. Then, as he became aware of the wetness of warm blood against his skin, he scrambled hurriedly to his feet. Gone now was the Irish Rover, the Happy Warrior

I had known throughout the past several weeks. Paddy's face was chalk white and oddly shrunken. He looked as if he was going to cry, or vomit, or do both.

One of the dead men lay with his face turned toward me. His eyes were open and as yet undimmed... and they were blue, like mine. This was no alien, this youth who must have been about my own age. Like me he sported a wisp of blonde moustache on his sunburned face—a face that was turning dusty yellow as his heart's blood flowed thickly from a chest that had been ripped asunder by a burst from Paddy's Thomson. Thrown on his back by the impact of the heavy slugs, he had fallen with his arms outflung in the way of children when they make angels in the snow. The woven gold stripe of a second lieutenant shone brightly on each sleeve.

Horses suddenly snorted, and I heard someone say:

"... coming in to surrender... what their sergeant says..."

Then Alex spoke. "What matter! It's war and they're likely lying anyway. Let's get on with it!"

The equipment we had captured made Alex as happy as a child with a basket of toys. Having set some of the men to pacify the horses, he ordered an ex-artillery corporal from Park's platoon to see if the two guns could be brought into action; and he put our company driver-mechanic to work attempting to resuscitate the old truck, which had stopped a bullet with its radiator.

God only knows what would have happened if these efforts had succeeded. Equipped with his own artillery, and with horse and motor transport, Alex might have struck so deeply into the heart of Sicily that we would never have emerged again. However, the guns had no sights, the truck was beyond emergency aid, and one of Park's sections which had gone forward on patrol hurriedly returned to report what sounded like enemy tanks approaching from the north. If the artillery pieces had been in order, Alex might have attempted to repel a tank attack; but as things stood he wisely, if reluctantly, decided to lead us eastward into the shelter of the beachhead.

We took the horses and prisoners with us, and for the rest of the day wandered "lost and lonely," as the poem goes, up and down winding, aimless tracks; hot, hungry and desperately thirsty. Just before dusk we found the rest of the Regiment resting in an olive grove northwest of Pachino. Alex went off to get his arm dressed, leaving us in a state of anxiety, for we were very much afraid he would be evacuated to a hospital ship waiting offshore. We need not have worried. Returning with his arm in a sling and a glint in his eye, he told us he had avoided evacuation by threatening to knock the medical officer's head off. "Think they can make me miss my chance?" he growled. "By God, they can damn well think again!"

OUR FIRST DAY of battle had been kinder to us than we could have hoped, but we were now to discover that combat is not necessarily the hardest face of war. Before dawn of July 11, we were chivvied out of exhausted slumber under the olive trees and ordered to move out of the beachhead.

First Division's sector had been defended by Italian coastal troops, ill-armed and ill-equipped. These units had quickly disintegrated, some of their men deliberately seeking captivity at our hands, others stripping off their battered uniforms in order to become instant civilians, while those who were willing to continue the war had fled into the hills. It now became our task to catch them before they could establish new defence positions.

As the sun rose high, the winding tracks became smoking arteries sending up dusty projections of themselves into the still air. The dust rose so thickly it was almost as if we were physically thrusting against its pall. It gathered on sweating faces where it hardened into a cracking crust. Our feet sank into it, as if into a tenuous slime. The heat was brutal—and there was no water. The sun became an implacable enemy and our steel helmets became brain furnaces. The weight of our personal equipment, together with weapons and extra ammunition, became almost intolerable.

The ship carrying our motor transport had been torpedoed off Malta, and so there was no alternative for us except foot-slogging. We marched along the verges, where there was no grass, only more of the eternal dust. Occasional Sherman tanks rumbled past, obliterating whole companies in a hanging shroud. Nevertheless, the attenuated brigade column, strung out over many miles, slowly worked its way upward into the hills.

There were occasional brief halts during which we could look back at the broad blue sweep of Pachino Bay dotted with minute ship models. But most of us just stared down at our steaming feet as we dragged at the incomparably bad issue cigarettes whose smoke was bitter and acrid in our parched mouths. Evening brought surcease from the heat but none from dust and thirst. The roads became steeper and exhaustion took its toll. Men began to drop out and were left behind. Other men slept on the move—a trick learned on English training schemes—and were guided by comrades who were themselves staggering with fatigue.

At midnight we passed through our first Italian town, but I have no memory of it except that there was a well in its central square—a well which had been sucked dry by the time we reached it. A few miles beyond this place, and some twenty miles from the starting point of the march, the Regiment finally halted. We staggered into the stony fields and collapsed. We were beyond caring about food. We died on the hard ground... and three hours later were goaded to our feet and set upon the road once more.

It was noon of July 12 before we halted again. By then we had marched nearly fifty miles and it was not within our strength to do more. Nevertheless, the pursuit of the retreating enemy could not wait and so a squadron of Shermans lumbered up; and like a group of somnambulists, we of Able Company clambered aboard the monsters to become the vanguard of the advance. To us those tanks were as heavenly chariots. On we rolled, passing through the deserted, stinking streets of the town of Giarratana until at midnight we came to a halt on the lip of a high plateau.

The agonizing march was at an end, but our ordeal was not. Before we could surrender to the stupor of exhaustion, we had to establish a defence perimeter by scraping rudimentary weapon pits in the rock-hard soil. We could hardly have cared less if we had been told to dig our own graves.

I have few coherent memories of that horrendous march... only hazed images, obscured as if by the perpetual dust itself.

... sprawling on my stomach during a too-brief pause on a bald hillside that shimmered under a destroying sun... Alex limping toward me, looming like a white rhinoceros, his voice cracking with drought... "What the blazes are you lying about for, Mowat? Look to your men's fcet!"

... seeing Corporal Mitchuk, that unamiable man, already burdened with his section's Bren gun, wordlessly slip an

anti-tank projector from the sagging shoulders of an unidentifiable ghost and stagger on with both weapons slung across
his sweat-soaked back.

... sitting, head bowed, on a rock so hot it scalded my backside, dully watching a tarantula which, disturbed by our invasion, was cautiously seeking safer shelter. Then a hand on my
shoulder and something thrust into my face... a water bottle containing an ounce or two of tepid, stinking fluid that I
sucked in as greedily as ever a baby did its mother's milk...
and Sergeant Bates's gravelly voice: "Take it easy, for Christ's
sake, that's all there is!"

... the certain knowledge that I could go no farther and the
equally certain knowledge that I must. Slyly slipping my officers' escape kit (to be opened only if one was captured) out of
my pocket, unscrewing the top of a tiny phial of Benzedrine
and forcing the tablets down the dry gulch of my throat.

... clinging to the smoke projector on a tank turret, the
metal so hot it seared my hand, and hearing the scream of
horror from a man in Eight Platoon as he lost his grip on the
sloping front of the following tank, and slid into the roaring
vortex of dust between its churning treads.

... thinking of being a fighter pilot, wheeling high and free
in the cool mercy of some northern sky... and a sudden flaming rage against my father for having inveigled me into the
clutches of the infantry—"The Queen of Battle!"

THAT WISTFUL DESIRE to be a pilot instead of a foot-slog-
ger was short-lived. Soon after dawn next day two Messerschmitts came screaming at us out of nowhere. They sprayed
the road that ran through Able Company's position with a
clattering flail of tracer... then flew straight into the massed

75

fire of a light anti-aircraft battery hidden in a roadside hollow. One of the German planes went into a hill behind us at three hundred miles an hour. The other staggered into an abrupt turn and scrambled desperately to gain altitude, but as it slid out of sight over a distant ridge it was trailing a long plume of greasy black smoke.

The eruption of anger against my father had amazed and frightened me, for I had not known that I carried within me any such smouldering resentment. But such is the resiliency of youth, and the perfidy of memory, that it had faded, together with most of the other miseries of our blistering march, into insignificance before we ended the forty-eight hours "at rest."

"At rest!" Ah, the unconscious humour of the military mind. Here is the way we took our ease.

Through most of the first day all of us—officers and men alike—sweated and swore over the obligatory task of hacking more weapon pits and deeper slit trenches into the flint-hard soil, equipped with nothing but entrenching tools—diminutive spades with foot-long handles that each man carried slung on his web belt. This we were forced to do despite the assurances of an armoured-car squadron, which had thrust fifteen miles beyond our position, that the enemy had abandoned the entire region.

The digging done, my next task was to distribute "compo" rations to my bone-weary, half-starved men who had subsisted up to this time on their emergency rations—the can of bully beef and two or three biscuits which each of us carried in our packs.

Designed by some chairborne genius in England, the compo pack consisted of a wooden crate containing everything fourteen men were supposed to require for twenty-four hours: hard-tack biscuits in lieu of bread; canned yellow wax, misleadingly labelled margarine; tins of M&V (unidentifiable scraps of fat and gristle mushed up with equally unidentifiable vegetables); canned processed cheese which tasted like, and may well have been, casein glue; powdered tea, milk and sugar, all ready mixed; turnip jam (laughingly labelled strawberry or raspberry); eight (count them) tiny hard candies for each man; seven India-made Victory cigarettes which, it was rumoured, were manufactured from the dung of sacred cattle; six squares of toilet paper per man (the surplus, if any, could be used to roll one's own cigarettes—if one had any tobacco); and one further item which caused more trouble than anything else—a twelve-ounce can of treacle pudding that was an irresistible object of desire to every one of us and the memory of which can still set me to salivating like a Pavlovian dog. Its appeal lay in the fact that it was soaked in molasses, and we were starving for sweet stuffs.

Dividing the contents of two compo packs into scrupulously equal portions for the thirty-three bodies in a full-strength platoon was no task for ordinary men. Because my non-commissioned officers were fully aware of this, it was impossible to pawn the distribution off on Sergeant Bates or even on a committee consisting of my three section corporals. Their sense of self-preservation was too keen. As Bates frankly told me:

"No bloody way you can please all those sons a bitches, and you short one of them on his treacle pudding and he'll likely shoot you in the back!"

Bates may have thought *my* back was armour-plated. In any event, dividing up the rations was the job I detested above all others.

On our first day of rest in Sicily I somehow fumbled through the distribution, after which we all slumped in a state of mindless exhaustion beside our slit trenches and glutched down our rations cold. We were not permitted to light even a tea fire in case a twirl of smoke might give away our position to the long-departed enemy.

The meal finished, we "stood-to" through the twilight hours, manning our weapons and ready to repel an enemy attack. After that, all hands except the guards were permitted to sleep. Despite our fatigue, sleep did not come easily, for we were wearing thin tropical kit (shorts and bush shirts) and had neither coats nor blankets. Since we had by then climbed a couple of thousand feet above sea level, the night was bitter chill. It was short, however, for at 0500 hours we had to stumble to our feet, buckle on our equipment and stand-to again, staring through glazed eyes into the dreary dawn, waiting for an enemy who did not come—*could* not come and did not *want* to come, being much too concerned with continuing his retreat.

Stand-to was one of several sacred rites that had been carried over from the First War. Throughout the whole of the Italian campaign, the Canadian fighting troops were required to stand-to at dusk and dawn whenever they were in the line, although never, in my experience, did the enemy prove so foolish as to attack at those times when we were so ritually prepared.

After stand-to on the morning of July 14, we were required to spend an hour cleaning our weapons before being allowed to eat our scanty breakfast. It seemed just possible we might then be allowed to take life easy for awhile, but at 0800 Alex called his platoon commanders together to tell us we were to be honoured by a visit from a VIP.

"Fall in for parade at 0930," he told us. "Meanwhile, get your men cleaned up. I want every one of them to be a credit to himself and to the Regiment."

I was frankly afraid to carry this news back to my platoon. In cowardly fashion I passed it on to Bates, who stared at me in outraged incredulity for a moment before letting fly a string of obscenities directed at the high command, for which any court-martial would have awarded him five years in prison. Nevertheless, when parade was finally called I found my men tidied up as well as circumstances would allow.

All save one. Doc Macdonald looked like a dissolute gnome who had spent an unwashed lifetime working in a combined flour mill and blast furnace. When I tasked him with his dreadful appearance, he blew his top.

"What the hell you expect? I got to spend most of my time cleaning up after you, like a dog with a dumb pup, and then you want me to turn out in dancing togs? Screw you *and* the bloody VIP."

It seemed best to leave Doc behind to mind the shop while we marched off to join the rest of the Regiment which was assembling in a natural amphitheatre a mile distant. Once there, we stood waiting, as Paddy Ryan put it: "For God to make his appearance out of a fiery cloud."

It was not God who came; it was his self-anointed deputy. General Bernard Montgomery, fabled commander of the Eighth Army, descended upon us in a long, open Bentley limousine. We came to attention, presented arms, and then were told to "gather round" while the ferret-faced little man in his black beret stood up on the back seat of his car waving an Egyptian flyswatter, and gave us the Word.

We were, he told us, first-rate troops who had done extremely well so far.

"But there's a big task ahead, my lads. The Eyeties are packing it in but Jerry is determined to hold on to Sicily. Our job is to toss him out! We'll do it ... yes, we'll do it! See him off, by Heavens! So keep up the good work, lads. I'll have my eye on you, never fear. Eighth Army always looks after its own!"

Then the unthinkable happened. From a rear rank a deep voice shouted:

"Where the hell's our beer ration then?"

The flyswatter twirled furiously and Montgomery grinned wolfishly.

"No beer. No room on the ships yet for anything but guns and ammo. First things first, you see? And while I'm on the subject, I strongly advise all of you to leave the Eyetie wine alone. Deadly stuff! Can make you blind, you know."

Lieutenant Colonel Sutcliffe hurriedly called the battalion to attention and the big staff car started up and drove away.

Although the visit had been an imposition on us, we were nevertheless so proud of being part of Monty's Eighth that the fulsome entry in that day's war diary was not entirely a false assessment:

... as a result of this stirring experience, all ranks were imbued with much added enthusiasm and an increased respect for this great commander.

All ranks? Not, I fear, Doc Macdonald.

PERHAPS BECAUSE HIGHER command could think of nothing else with which to plague us, we were allowed the afternoon to ourselves. Corporal Mitchuk and several of his cronies disobeyed a strict injunction to remain inside our defence perimeter and slipped quietly away. They returned an hour or two later to prepare themselves a dinner of "scrounged" chicken and goat, washed down by quantities of acrid red wine of a quality which seemed to confirm General Montgomery's opinion of Sicilian vino.

I was permitted to share this meal and did so gratefully; nor did I ask any questions about its provenance. Division had ruled that scrounging was a version of looting, and looting was forbidden under penalties of as much as ten years' imprisonment. This was grossly unfair, for while looting was outright theft, scrounging normally entailed some kind of barter. Sergeant Bates spoke for every fighting man when he proclaimed:

"If they clobber us for scrounging they can kiss their goddamn army by-byes. If we gotta live on the issue crap they feed us, any ten-year-old Wop with his hands tied behind his back'll be able to kick the living Jesus out of us!"

I SPENT MOST of that strangely quiescent afternoon writing letters.

This country is absolutely foul. Dry as a bone, hot as hell during the day, and icy cold at night. The whole place looks like the North Dakota badlands. Towns are few and scruffy, always perched on hills like ravens' nests, and the stink has been collecting in them since Year One. The civvies are dirt poor and look half starved. The Eyetie soldiers are crack troops though—they crack every time we hit them. We've made fantastic progress but may slow down a bit now because the rumour is that Jerry is moving south to meet us, and he is a horse of another colour. But not to worry, we'll light a rocket under his tail too!

Most of the men dozed the hot afternoon away in the thin shade of the ubiquitous olive trees. For them it was enough simply not to be on the move; but off by himself A.K. Long sat reading, his back to a gnarled tree bole, deep in the world of Herman Melville. I drifted past him, dearly wanting to stop and chat but afraid of a rebuff.

After supper the platoon commanders were called to Company Headquarters, there to find a battle-hungry Alex.

"Fifty-first Div's bumped the Jerries at Vizzini," he told us with delight. "Soon as they clear the town the Regiment's to move through and take the lead. Praise be we'll get *real* action now!"

Vizzini was nearly forty miles ahead and we moved up to it on borrowed transport as the German defenders were abandoning the town. At 0600 on July 15 the order came for us to push forward on the German rearguard's heels.

This was a motorized thrust headed by Baker Company clinging to a squadron of Shermans. Able followed with two platoons jammed into trucks, led by my platoon rumbling along directly behind the tanks in three of the lightly armoured, open-topped tracked vehicles known as Bren carriers. The rest of the battalion, accompanied by more tanks and a squadron of Priests (25-pounder guns mounted on tank chassis) stretched out for more than a mile astern.

It was another glaring day. The arid hills loomed desolate on every side while to the north the white cone of Etna shimmered in distant splendour. The road looped and laboured over a wild landscape. Villages of prehistoric origin hung on their pinnacles of sun-blasted rock. Decaying fortresses—relics of wars that had raged through Sicily for three millennia—looked down upon yet one more invading army. Brown fields burned under the smoking dust stirred by our column, and here and there little groups of desiccated peasants straightened bent backs and stared as impassively at our military might as they probably had at the guns and armour of the retreating Germans short hours earlier.

There was a tingling expectancy upon us, for though none could know where or when the enemy would be encountered, the column was committed to roll ponderously on until it "bumped" the German defences.

The first encounter was anticlimactic. An approaching pall of dust resolved itself into a small truck of unfamiliar make hurtling out of the north at breakneck speed. It did not slacken pace until it seemed about to collide with the leading Sherman, which had stopped and was tracking the approaching vehicle with its 75-mm cannon. There was a shriek of brakes as the stranger skidded to a halt. Then followed a moment of absolute immobility while we stared at this apparition. Its occupants stared back, dumbfounded, into the muzzles of scores of weapons aimed directly at them. The moment ended when two German privates in the khaki uniforms of the Afrika Korps leapt down to the road, hands thrown high in panic-stricken surrender. Drivers of a ration truck, they had misread their map and lost their way... a thing that was easy enough to do in Sicily.

Having unexpectedly and bloodlessly taken our first German prisoners, we moved on. The lead tanks climbed a high saddle and paused on the crest, appearing to sniff suspiciously as their out-thrust cannon swung slowly back and forth. Below us lay a flat and formless plain stretching to the foot of a massive escarpment some three miles distant upon whose crest rose the crenelated silhouette of a town.

Cautiously the tanks lumbered down the slope to the valley floor. Dust plumes rose high and straight in the still air, proclaiming our approach. Slowly we rumbled across the parched plain and began the ascent of a switchback road that zigzagged up the escarpment. The lead tank, with most of a platoon of Baker aboard, had reached the outskirts of the hillcrest town when the crew of a hidden anti-tank gun sprang the trap the Germans had so carefully contrived for us.

The town of Grammichele was defended by two infantry battalions of the elite Hermann Göring Division supported by tanks and artillery. At the crash of the first shot all of these forces opened fire on the nakedly exposed column stretching across the valley below them.

Standing in the unroofed gunner's compartment of the lead carrier, I had been bird-watching when the battle started, my binoculars focussed on a pair of red-tailed kites soaring on the updrafts from the escarpment. As I tried to hold the big birds in the shaky circle of my glasses, they went into a sudden dive, sliding swiftly out of sight. I heard a distant snarling bark, a whining scream, and then a stunning crash as a shell burst a few yards away from the carrier. Shrapnel and stone splinters sprayed against the vehicle's thin armour. It gave a skittish little leap, like a frightened horse, and slid sideways into the ditch.

Half-deafened, shrouded in smoke and dust, I was so flabbergasted that I remained standing with binoculars in hand until, very distantly it seemed, I heard Corporal Hill yelling.

"Bail out! Bail out, for Jesus' sake!"

Quite casually I obeyed, and only when I stood on the roadside did I become fully aware of the cacophony of sound and fury which had exploded on all sides.

Doc Macdonald grabbed my arm and together we rolled into the ditch behind the carrier. My other two sections had already abandoned their vehicles and were sprinting away from the road. Doc and I scrambled to our feet and joined the rout—just seconds before two of the carriers brewed up. CRASH-*Whooosh!*—CRASH-*Whooosh!* Their gasoline tanks flamed skyward and two immense black and golden globes blossomed over us.

Panting, dishevelled and with faces blackened by the explosions, Doc and I tumbled into a gravelly depression some fifty yards off the road where the rest of the platoon had already taken cover. The hollow gave us all-too-little protection from shell bursts, but it did provide a fine view of the action.

From the crest and forward slopes of the mile-long escarpment the Germans were firing down upon our column with everything they had—and they seemed to have just about everything. During my time as battalion intelligence officer, I had thoroughly boned up on German weapons, but until this hour I had never actually seen or heard the real thing. Now I was delighted to discover that I could identify most of them. It was a discovery which excited me almost as much as if I had stumbled on a batch of new bird species.

A covey of mortar shells fluted overhead and crashed into the road. "81-mm medium mortars!" I cried at Bates who had crawled up beside me. He only grunted, his attention riveted on the spectacle of the lead Sherman brewing up in a dense black plume of oily smoke at the entrance to the town. Behind us all the soft-skinned vehicles of the convoy now stood abandoned. A thunderous explosion made me turn in time to see a three-ton ammunition truck going up in a stupendous display of fireworks. Just then an incredibly rapid *whickety-whick-whick-whick* snapped through the air over our heads.

"Hey, Bates," I shouted. "That must be an MG-42! A lot faster than our Brens!"

"Yeah, a real pisscutter," Bates replied sardonically. "But you better keep your fucking head down or you'll lose the bloody thing!" he added, as I raised myself to watch four streaks of brilliant orange sparks floating toward us from an enfilading position on the left of the escarpment. Rapidly swelling to balls of fire they speeded up mysteriously as they grew larger, then they flashed overhead to burst like a string of giant firecrackers on the back wall of our hollow.

For a moment I was puzzled, then I had it!

Four-barrelled Flakvierling light anti-aircraft mount, depressed for ground action...

"Mother of God, what's that!" Doc yelled as an ear-splitting whiplash of sound ended in a savage crunch that showered us with grit and gravel.

I had already heard this one, for it had been the nemesis of our carriers. It was the infamous "Eighty-eight"—the high-velocity cannon which served the Germans in a multiple role as anti-tank, anti-aircraft or anti-personnel artillery. In days to come its very name would become freighted with acute apprehension, but on that bright morning as we lay before the citadel of Grammichele I was naively admiring of its spectacular performance. Not so Doc.

"Fuck this racket," he muttered with conviction. "They going to throw *that* kind of stuff around, I'm going to dig myself a hole!"

This was a sound idea and we were all soon scrabbling at the hard ground with our entrenching tools, our efforts given greater impetus by a battery of 105-mm gun-howitzers which opened fire from behind the Grammichele ridge. The heavy shells fell in salvos of three or four, shaking the ground with a horrendous CRUMP... CRUMP... CRUMP!

By now our column had recovered somewhat from the first shock of ambush and was beginning to fight back. The British Priests deployed and soon the throaty roar of their 25-pounders firing over open sights was followed by a familiar snarl as their shells tunnelled over us to erupt in bursts of flame along the face of the escarpment. The reserve squadron of Shermans rattled forward, went into hull-down positions behind some little knolls, and the wicked bark of their 75s joined the swelling din. Even we of the infantry, now scattered in little groups all over the flat plain, began to reply with rifle and Bren fire aimed in the general direction of the unseen enemy.

Although it was a spirited reaction, it would hardly have saved the column from decimation if the enemy had only been able to keep us at arm's length. But in his desire to lure as many as possible of the leading tanks right onto the muzzles of his hidden guns, he had waited too long before opening fire. Two tanks were knocked out immediately; but the rest, finding themselves in a trap from which there was no retreat, charged straight ahead with such impetuosity that they overran the

German guns before the gunners could reload, then rumbled on unhindered to the shelter of a row of houses. Once there the Baker Company platoons leapt off and, covered by fire from the tanks, scuttled forward into the centre of the town where, by their mere presence, they threatened the enemy's sole avenue of retreat down a switchback road running to the north. Finding themselves in danger of being trapped in their turn, the Germans began to abandon their positions.

"When the first Sherman bought it," one of Baker's platoon commanders told me later, "I figured we were all gone geese! We cleared off from the tanks like fleas leaving a drowning dog and lit out for the nearest shelter, which happened to be the town. My God, those stone houses sure looked good! There wasn't any orders given. We just went charging into the place hell-a-whooping and I never even noticed if there was any Jerries trying to stop us. Next thing I knew we were holed up in a big *casa* overlooking a crossroads where the whole son-of-a-bitching German army seemed to be on the move— tanks, armoured cars, motorcycles, trucks—the works! Did we *shoot* at them? Not bloody likely! We were so goddamn glad to see them go we'd probably have cheered them on if we hadn't been scared they'd clobber us!"

When, a little less than an hour after the first shot had been fired, the enemy fire began to wither and fall away, those of us pinned down in the valley were, in our ignorance and arrogance, not at all surprised. It had taken a little longer to give Jerry the boot than it would have taken to dislodge a bunch of Eyeties, but we had never been in doubt as to the eventual outcome. In truth, my crowd was somewhat disappointed it was all over so quickly and that we had had no real piece of the action. It did not occur to any of us that, through a miscalculation on the part of the enemy commander, we might have escaped destruction by the skin of our teeth. Such was the measure of our innocence!

The battle of Grammichele ended just before noon. A group of wounded tank troopers sat stoically smoking beside a stone wall, waiting for an ambulance to reach them, as I wandered into the town in company with Al Park and Paddy Ryan. With professional interest we examined the armoured vehicles and guns the enemy had abandoned in his precipitate retreat. We joined numbers of our men looking for souvenirs while some of our drivers tentatively started up uninjured German trucks with which to replace the vehicle casualties we had suffered.

Relieved by another battalion of the role of advance guard, we had a few hours free to savour our success, while the rest of 1st Division rolled slowly past. The commanding general stopped to congratulate us and to tell us we were the first Canadians to fight a land battle with the Germans since Dieppe. Our signal victory, he said proudly, was only a token of greater victories ahead.

This was heady stuff, and so was a wicker-covered demi-john of vino Al's platoon had liberated. He and I collected a water bottle full as our share and went off to savour it in the scanty shade of an old fig tree.

"Nothing much to it, eh?" Al nonchalantly waved the bottle toward the town above us.

"Piece of cake!" I replied. "Here's to the old Plough Jockeys!"

Al passed the bottle and looked at me for a long moment as though of two minds whether or not to speak. Then:

"How did you *really* feel, Squib, when all that crap started to plonk down? Bit of a shaker, wasn't it?"

"Sort of," I admitted with some reluctance. "Scared me for a minute or two 'til I saw it wasn't doing much damage. Jerry's got some red-hot toys all right, but you got to know how to use them and I don't think he's all that good... Yeah... it was a surprise, but I didn't get the wind up, if that's what you're wondering."

In truth, the encounter had been too sudden, too brief and, on the whole, too harmless to incubate the latent seeds of fear. Yet something must have been alerted in the depths of my subconscious, else why would I have written to a friend in Canada that very afternoon:

> It was exciting as hell, and I didn't lose a single man, though I guess that kind of luck can't last forever. It makes you think, you know, when you see a twenty-ton tank with four guys in it go whoof in one big burst of flame...

We bivouacked in a relatively green valley near Grammichele until evening of the following day and during this respite had our first real contact with the *Sicilianos*. Most of what we saw we did not like. The homes of these desperately poor hill-dwellers were hovels, and the people themselves—small, dark, reserved, leather-faced and listless—seemed to merit nothing more than benevolent contempt. Nevertheless, I was surprised to hear one of my own men, whose parents had been Italian emigrants to Canada, condemn them with undisguised disgust:

"*Sicilianos!* Aaagh! They're a bunch of dirty bandits... lazy bums!"

His was an attitude which somehow seemed to sanction making these people's meagre possessions fair game. In any event, many of their pitiful little orchards (a handful of fig trees, pears or pomegranates) and garden plots (mostly melons and gourds) were casually looted. However, the loot did the thieves little good, for the clouds of flies rising from human and animal excrement implanted dysentery germs on almost everything that came out of the ground. "Gyppy gut," as Eighth Army veterans called it, soon became epidemic amongst us too.

Late on July 16 we were again on the move as part of a fearfully slow and tedious convoy snaking and writhing its way higher and higher into increasingly arid mountain country. The roads were lean-gutted and tortuous and, to make matters worse, the retreating Germans had systematically demolished every culvert and bridge so that traffic had to slow to the merest crawl at a multitude of rough diversions. Nevertheless, by noon next day we had reached the recently captured town of Piazza Amerina.

Traffic congestion in the narrow, winding streets halted the truck carrying me and my platoon in the main square. Spotting a public water faucet I nipped out of the cab to see if its contents were drinkable; for if we had learned one solid lesson so far in Sicily, it was never to miss a chance to fill one's water bottle. When a Royal Engineer sergeant assured me the water had been tested and was potable, I yelled at my section corporals to grab some water bottles from their men.

The four of us were crowded around the ornate cast-iron spigot when I became aware of the presence of a tall, dignified officer in serge dress uniform complete with shiny brass buttons and gleaming Sam Browne belt. He was as remarkable an apparition in that outfit, time and place, as a king in a chicken coop. Assuming that he must be some very senior variety of staff officer, I glanced at him nervously, expecting a reprimand for having let my men leave the truck; but when he spoke it was to quite a different point.

"I say, old man, would you mind awfully if I took your photograph?"

The question seemed so out of place that even Mitchuk grinned, and I heard Hill ask under his breath: "Jesus, have we got ourselves a movie star?" I was too nonplussed to reply, and our driver was gunning his engine as a signal that the convoy was moving on, but I must have nodded acquiescence. In any case, a picture of me, dust-caked and clad in stained and torn shorts and bush shirt that had not been changed since leaving the *Derbyshire,* eventually graced the august pages of the *London Illustrated News.*

I had encountered my first British war correspondent.

We had gone only a few miles beyond Piazza Amerina when we were signalled off the road. We piled stiffly down from the trucks and broke out the compo rations, but before we could eat, the officers were told to report to Alex Campbell who was breathing fire and brimstone, his eyes glaring as fiercely as ever despite or perhaps because of the pain his wounded arm must have been giving him.

"Third Brigade's been stopped about six miles up the road," he told us exultantly. "Whole advance is bogged down and there's just one way to bust it open. First Brigade's going to make a right hook through the mountains and cut the highway behind the Jerries at a place called Valguarnera. Find it on your maps... got it? Right. Well, the brigadier has picked the Hasty Pees to do the job... and the co's picked Able Company to lead the way."

DUSK HAD FALLEN before Lieutenant Colonel Sutcliffe issued his operation order. It was a tall one! In darkness, and without prior reconnaissance, we were to feel our way across many miles of mountainous wasteland, descend upon the German-held town of Valguarnera, cut the road in front of it and then, without benefit of tanks or heavy weapons, drive out the enemy garrison.

We platoon commanders had precious little time to study our maps, which were badly blurred copies of sketchy Italian originals. What little we could glean from the spider's web of contour lines which covered them made it clear we would be traversing such a manic confusion of gorges and pinnacles that even the native Sicilians seemed to have left the region trackless. At any rate, the maps showed not so much as a dotted line which might have indicated the presence of even a goat path along our projected route.

Although it was vital that we should travel as light as possible, our bare essentials still amounted to a formidable load. Each private carried his rifle and a hundred rounds of .303 in a bandolier slung across his shoulder. The two large pouches on the front of his webbing bulged with four 30-round magazines for his section's Bren. Several Mills, or anti-tank, grenades were clipped to his shoulder straps. Hanging from his belt were his entrenching tool, water bottle and bayonet. His small pack was stuffed with a rubberized groundsheet (intended to serve either as a shelter or as a rain cape), a couple of cans of bully beef, a handful of hardtack biscuits; and such oddments as cigarettes, tea and powdered milk were squeezed into the twin halves of his mess tin. Most men were additionally burdened with cartons of 2-inch mortar bombs or anti-tank projectiles. Nobody, including officers, was packing less than sixty pounds.

Able Company moved off in darkness and almost at once we found ourselves adrift in a maze of cliffs and canyons. Because of my presumed expertise as a map reader, I was delegated to lead the way but I stopped so often and made so many false starts that Alex impatiently took over the lead himself— with no better luck. Growling his frustration he paused every few minutes to study the map in the dim glow of a hooded flashlight until finally he was forced to accept the fact that it was useless to us.

The failure of the maps left us with only one alternative: to steer a compass course direct for Valguarnera. This proved extremely difficult since we could not go in any direction for more than twenty or thirty yards without being confronted either by an unscalable cliff or an impassable ravine.

Nevertheless, up and down and back and forth we went, stumbling into each other or into rocks or gnarled clumps of brush as we zigzagged to and fro in an infuriating parody of children playing blindman's buff. Despite the chill of the night (we were approaching an altitude of 4,000 feet), our thin cotton clothes were soon running wet with sweat.

After we had spent some hours blundering blindly about, a crescent moon emerged above a line of crenelated cliffs. We blessed it fervently, for without its help we never would have escaped from that lunatic jumble. However, the moon revealed more than just the shape of a tortured landscape—it also revealed the fact that nobody was following in Able Company's footsteps.

Alex at once sent me scurrying to the rear to re-establish contact, but I could find no sign of the rest of the battalion.

The other three rifle companies together with Battalion Headquarters seemed to have vanished into thin air. The realization that we were on our own did not seem to perturb Alex much; on the contrary, I think he was secretly delighted at the opportunity to engage in a private war against the Germans.

But first we had to win our battle with an inanimate enemy. Hour after hour we struggled on, climbing innumerable cliffs and slithering into cactus-filled gullies, with never a sign that human beings had ever been this way before. We were near total exhaustion when, puffing like a grampus, Alex finally resigned the lead to Paddy Ryan, and shortly thereafter Paddy fell over a mule.

The mule was sleeping on a path which we soon discovered led to a stone hovel a few hundred yards away. The world was found again!

Able was accompanied that night by Lieutenant Pat Amoore, a suave and debonair young man from British Intelligence Corps temporarily attached to the Regiment as an interpreter. Because he looked and acted like a Noel Coward creation, he was scorned by some of the other subalterns. "Full of piss and wind!" was how Paddy Ryan contemptuously described him; but I rather liked Amoore. Beneath his impeccable English overlay, he was of Italian stock and spoke the language as a native. Now he was called upon to roust out the inhabitants of the hovel and find out where the devil we were or, better yet, where Valguarnera was.

Waking the ancient couple who inhabited the place was easy, but dealing with them, once awake, turned out to be something else.

Terrified by this invasion of their remote mountain canyon, the old woman began screaming like a banshee while her husband, who had emerged from his bed naked as a babe, hysterically beseeched the Lord Almighty to spare their lives.

We were so appalled by the noise these two old folk together with the mule (which was braying to its own gods for help) were making, and so fearful it would alarm the Germans, wherever they might be, that we abandoned the interrogation and fled down the newly discovered trail—fled straight onto the muzzles and cocked weapons of Charley Company which, being also lost and lonely, and equally horrified by the demented caterwauling we had unleashed, was preparing to defend itself to the death against God only knew what terrors of the night.

Such was the relief of both companies at having found one another that it was some time before Alex and Rolly Cleworth, Charley Company's commander, could get us organized and on the move again.

The track now led steeply downhill toward the north and as the false dawn began to silhouette the eastern peaks we reached a paved road. Cautiously we scouted some distance along it in both directions but saw nobody, nor could we find any indication of what road it was or where it led. However, one thing was certain: as the deep imprint of tank treads testified, it had been in recent heavy use by military traffic that could have been none of ours.

It was time to make a halt. Across the road from us stood a dome-shaped hill whose slopes, terraced and stone-walled, seemed to offer good concealment. Covered by Bren gunners, our six platoons nipped smartly across the broken pavement and climbed the rising ground to take up an all-round defence from which we could command the road in both directions.

We were startled to find that the hill was already occupied by several score of refugees who had come here seeking safety from the fighting between 3rd Brigade and the Germans to the westward.

Pat Amoore discovered from these frightened farm folk that Valguarnera lay only a mile away, though hidden from our view by an intervening ridge, and that it was full of *Tedeschi*—barbarians, as the Germans were known to the Italians. They also told him that the road was the main lateral highway to Catania and was much used by German military traffic.

By guess and by God we had accomplished the first part of our task. However, we could not report our success to the rest of the battalion—or to anyone else for that matter—because our pack radios, which worked reasonably well over short distances and level ground, were useless in this mountainous terrain. Neither could we hope to obtain the support of friendly troops or of artillery. Under these circumstances, even Alex Campbell was unwilling to risk our small force in a frontal attack upon the town. He and Cleworth concluded that, having cut the road which linked the German forces to their own rear areas, the best thing we could do was stay where we were and try to keep it cut.

Dawn had broken and the great white sun ballooning over the far mountains began to banish the night's chill. My eyes hung heavy, and drowsily I heard a murmur of women's voices from the group of refugees. Then my eyes closed and I dreamed of summer sun on a sandy beach where a group of slender girls were begging me to join them in an erotic dance. As I swam slowly toward them through air which had become cool water, the dream suddenly exploded in a crashing staccato of machine-gun and rifle fire.

I leapt to my feet to find the road no longer empty. Six immense, green-painted trucks were grinding to a halt below us. As I stared, incredulous, the lead truck nosed ponderously into the ditch, canted slowly on its side and spilled out two or three dozen grey-clad soldiers. Now I was screaming at my men, some of whom were still drugged with sleep, wildly urging the Bren gunners into action.

Over a hundred and fifty German infantrymen were packed into those six trucks. They had been driving all night, en route to reinforce their comrades who were holding up 3rd Brigade's advance, and most of them must have been drowsing or asleep when they were engulfed in gunfire.

For a moment I was distracted by Sharon and Robinson, that pair of usually phlegmatic farm boys, clamouring to know if they should bring our anti-tank projector into action. Then a furious bellow made me turn to see Alex Campbell launching himself down the slope. He was holding a Bren tucked under his one good arm and firing quick bursts as he ran. Although a spare mag was clenched between his teeth, he was still able to roar like a maddened minotaur.

For precious seconds our fire grew ragged as we stared at Alex, appalled and awed by what he was doing. A few of the Germans tried to make use of the respite to bring rifles and Schmeisser machine pistols into play. Alex was by then only a few yards from the nearest of them and I momentarily expected to see his mighty bulk come crashing to the ground. We all must have shared that fear, for suddenly every man in the two companies began to fire again as fast as he could load. The rattle and roar of small arms and grenades rose to a crescendo... and the stretch of road below us became a slaughterhouse.

Alex concentrated his berserk fury on a single truck, and when he had finished firing into it from a range of a dozen yards, his consuming hatred of the enemy must surely have been sated. Within that truck twenty or more Germans writhed and died.

Meanwhile, soldiers from the other trucks were desperately trying to bail out through a thickening curtain of bullets, grenades and mortar bombs. Not many reached the dubious shelter of the roadside ditches, and most of those who did were wounded. As they and the few others who survived began making frantic efforts to surrender, the firing petered out and soon little groups of our men began herding prisoners off the road and up the hill.

Guarded by Corporal Hill's section with rifles at the ready, Amoore and I descended to the road to gather intelligence. This consisted mostly of counting the dead and wounded and of searching through blood-soaked tunics for unit identifications—documents and *Soldbuchs* (the German version of our paybooks). But after a time I could no longer stand the stench and sight, and left Pat alone to the gory chore.

It was not the dead that distressed me most—it was the German wounded. There were a great many of these, and most seemed to have been hard hit. We could do almost nothing for them. We had no medical supplies to spare, or even any water. One of their medical orderlies was among the handful of uninjured prisoners but he too was helpless for he had neither drugs nor field dressings.

One ghastly vignette from that shambles haunts me still: the driver of a truck hanging over his steering wheel and hiccupping great gouts of cherry-pink foam through a smashed windscreen, to the accompaniment of a sound like a slush pump sucking air as his perforated lungs laboured to expel his own heart's blood...in which he was slowly drowning.

Shortly after I returned to the company position a subaltern, who shall be nameless, suggested that the best thing we could do for the wounded Germans was to put them out of their misery. When this was received with hostility by the rest of us, he tried to justify himself.

"Goddamn it, they'll only bleed to death or die of thirst. Surely to Christ it'd be kinder to put a bullet through their heads!"

"That'll be enough of that!" ·

Alex, who had come up unseen behind us, was flushed and furious.

"There'll be *no* killing prisoners! Try anything like that and I'll see you court-martialled on a murder charge!"

The anomaly of hearing such sentiments voiced by a man who had just butchered twenty or thirty Germans did not strike me at the time. It does now. The line between brutal murder and heroic slaughter flickers and wavers... and becomes invisible.

ALTHOUGH WE HAD no way of knowing it, Dog and Baker companies had also managed to reach the lateral road several miles to the west of the town. Here they used their anti-tank weapons to knock out a number of German vehicles, including an armoured half-track towing an Eighty-eight. As a result of our twin thrusts the German position in front of 3rd Brigade had now been isolated; but we had stirred up a veritable hornet's nest in Valguarnera.

Shortly before 1000 hours a group of trucks moved cautiously eastward down the highway toward us but halted under cover half a mile away, and soon thereafter we were being attacked by a couple of companies of infantry supported by 81-mm mortars. This assault fell mostly on Charley Company and was beaten off with losses to us of two men killed and three wounded.

The lull that followed was short-lived. A troop of 12-cm heavy mortars began dropping 35-pound bombs among our all-too-shallow slit trenches. Simultaneously a number of armoured cars began to edge down the road firing 20-mm cannon and machine guns to cover yet another infantry attack. And shortly thereafter the crashing impact of a 105-mm shell gave us the bad news that a German artillery battery was ranging on us. This was too much for the Sicilian refugees who scattered like a gaggle of barnyard fowl and fled full tilt down the road, hastened on their way by some desultory rifle fire from the Germans who may, just conceivably, have mistaken them for some of us.

Had we been able to call for artillery fire ourselves, we might have held out a little longer, but our supply of small-arms ammo, mortar bombs and grenades was already perilously depleted, and there was also the certainty that if we stayed where we were we would eventually be surrounded. Consequently, Alex, as senior company commander, reluctantly ordered our withdrawal.

His reluctance was not shared by me. It was not hard to imagine what the Germans might do to any Canadians they captured—once they had seen the carnage we had made of their lorried infantry. Charley Company withdrew first; and when it came my turn to lead my platoon on a dash across the bullet-swept road and up the exposed slopes on the far side, I moved as if with winged feet.

I had not long gained the shelter of a rocky knoll some two hundred yards from the road and well above it—and had just finished siting my Brens to provide covering fire for the following platoons—when Alex plumped down beside me.

"I've sent Charley on ahead," he grunted. "They've taken the prisoners and the worst of our wounded and left us all their ammo. We'll stick it out as long as we damn well can... Try to keep those bastards from using the road..." He nodded toward Valguarnera from which direction yet another convoy of trucks had appeared, escorted this time by several tanks. "But you'll be rearguard when we *have* to quit."

At first our new position was not so bad. The enemy, milling about in the valley, was uncertain of our exact location and so his fire, though growing in volume all the time, remained relatively ineffective. Shortage of ammunition restricted our response to sniping and occasional bursts from a Bren, so it was difficult for him to spot us.

Our worst enemy on that sun-baked slope was thirst. All our water bottles had long since been drained and we had become so thick-tongued and dry-mouthed that talking required a painful effort. I could not tolerate a cigarette, even though I yearned desperately for one. However, if things were uncomfortable for the rest of us, they were ten times worse for our wounded, of whom Able Company now had nearly a dozen.

At this point Alex gathered his four subalterns—Paddy Ryan, Al Park, myself and Pat Amoore—in a fold of ground out of view of the Germans.

"I want an officer to take a party back down into the valley and get water," he said bluntly. "Who'll it be?"

I glanced surreptitiously at Park and Ryan, and found them covertly glancing my way. None of us said a word, for we all three were sure a descent into the valley would be tanta-mount to suicide.

It was Pat Amoore who, in his perfectly accented English, broke the impasse.

"Right oh, Skippah! I'll have a go. Hate to be idle, don't you know?"

He took with him only a Sten gunner and two riflemen, and within an hour they were back, staggering under a load of dripping water bottles which they had filled at a farm well—*after* surprising and killing several Germans in the courtyard. As we three Canadian subalterns gulped down our share of that precious stuff, we were also eating crow.

By 1400 the Germans had assembled enough guns, men and armour below us to be able to launch a battalion assault. The time had come for us to move along. Alex banged me on the shoulder with one ham of a hand and pushed his flare pis-tol at me with the other.

"Okay, Squib, we're pulling out. Nine Platoon with the wounded'll go first. Then Eight. Al will go to ground just over the crest to cover your withdrawal. He's got six rounds of mor-tar smoke—all there is left. The wounded'll slow us down so we'll need all the head start we can get. Stick it out as long as you can. When you have to leave, fire one red flare to let Al know you're on your way."

Alex left us Nine Platoon's three Brens to free their crews from the weight so they could help with the wounded. Six light machine guns gave me a lot of fire power... or would have done except that we only had one or two magazines remaining for each gun.

Wriggling forward to the edge of the knoll, I passed the word to shoot at anything that moved—but to make every bullet count. Behind me I could hear stones rattling as Eight and Nine platoons broke cover and began their rush up the steep slopes. Instantly the metallic hail from an MG-42 swept over our heads in vicious pursuit of our retreating comrades.

I had my binoculars to my eyes at that moment and by the sheerest fluke glimpsed a flicker of flame and a filmy wisp of smoke coming from a pile of brush on the far side of the road. Mitchuk was lying next to me behind his section's Bren, and I grabbed his arm and tried to make him see what I had seen but he could not locate the target. After a moment he rolled over and pushed the butt of the gun toward me.

"*You* take 'em, Junior!" he said . . . and grinned.

The feel of the Bren filled me with the same high excitement that had been mine when, as a boy during October days in Saskatchewan, I had raised my shotgun from the concealment of a bulrush blind and steadied it on an incoming flight of greenhead mallards.

There was a steady throbbing against my shoulder as the Bren hammered out a burst. A stitching of dust spurts appeared in front of the patch of brush and walked on into it. I fired burst after burst until the gun went silent with a heavy *clunk* as the bolt drove home on an empty chamber. Quickly Mitchuk slapped off the empty magazine and rammed a fresh one into place.

"Give 'em another!" he yelled exultantly. "You're onto the fuckers good!"

Maybe I was. It is at least indisputable that after I had emptied the second magazine there was no further firing nor any sign of life from the brush pile. On the other hand, I never actually saw a human target, so I cannot be haunted by the memory of men lying dead or dying behind their gun. And for that I am grateful.

Clumps of 81-mm mortar bombs were now beginning to flute down upon the slopes, feeling for us and filling the air with the whine and whizz of metal fragments and rock splinters. Far down the road a Mk III tank cranked the muzzle of its cannon up to maximum elevation and began spitting 50-mm shells at us. Our situation was becoming uncomfortably hot in every way, and I looked anxiously behind to see how the other two platoons were faring. To my vast relief, they had vanished over the crest and were out of reach of directed enemy fire. But a glance at my watch revealed that they had been gone a mere ten minutes—not enough time to put a safe distance between themselves and any pursuit the Germans might mount once Seven Platoon had withdrawn.

And oh, how I ached to go! The German mortar and machine-gun fire was steadily intensifying. Three of my men had already been hit, though not seriously, thank God! We were just about out of ammo. The brass handle of the flare pistol was burning my palm. I held it away from me, and suddenly there was a *poof* and a red flare burst overhead. I was unaware that I had pulled the trigger.

The flare was still burning when the first smoke bomb from Al Park's 2-inch mortar plummeted in front of our knoll and coils of white smoke began to shroud us from the enemy's view. Another bomb and another fell and the smoke thickened.

"Get the hell out of here!" I screamed at the top of my lungs, and the platoon took off like a clutch of gophers scuttling to escape a pursuing coyote. It was every man for himself, but luck was with us for every man made it over the crest before the smoke from the last of Al's bombs began to dissipate.

The return journey through the mountains to our own lines was an anticlimax—more of the same sort of thing we had endured on the outward march, although made somewhat easier because we could at least see our way, and also because we were sustained against an overwhelming fatigue by the afterglow of a battle well fought and won.

All during that long afternoon and into the night, little groups of weary men staggered out of the hills, until by midnight the Regiment was almost whole again—except for the dead, and the wounded whom we had left hidden in a mountain valley guarded by one of Charley Company's platoons. They were brought out next morning by our first-aid men who performed a small miracle in manoeuvring their laden stretchers through that formidable wasteland.

That night Field Marshal Albert Kesselring, commander-in-chief of the German armies in southern Europe, radioed his daily situation report to Berlin:

> ... and near Valguarnera troops trained in mountain fighting have been encountered. They are believed to belong to the 1st Canadian Division. Our forces have successfully disengaged from action with them.

Able Company was allowed to rest most of the next day, but late in the afternoon Alex sent me to Battalion Headquarters to deliver our casualty list to Jimmy Bird, the adjutant. Jimmy's inevitable nickname, Dicky, fitted him admirably, for he was the ultimate brood mother, eternally—and usually disapprovingly—fussing and clucking over us as if we were a flock of bird-brained kids.

Since I seldom had a chance to get near BHQ anymore, I took the opportunity to try and pump him about impending plans. He was uncommunicative.

"*Really*, Squib," he replied primly, "how should I know what's going on? It's not *my* job to set the world on fire! *That's* up to the high-priced help. All *I* do is put the pieces together after you silly characters get everything mucked up!"

Grinning, I went in search of the Intelligence Section truck—the Brain Wagon. This was the first time I had visited my old section since being posted to Seven Platoon, and that seemed like years ago. Two of the scouts greeted me with exaggerated salutes and a cheerful, "Welcome back!"

"Battle" Cockin, the English intelligence officer who had replaced me, was under the truck's canvas canopy, bending over a big situation map covered with transparent plastic. He was busily marking our own and enemy positions on the slick surface with red and blue grease pencils. I peered over his shoulder and for the first time since landing in Sicily was able to get some idea of what was happening in the "big picture."

The Italians having virtually given up, and the four German divisions then in Sicily being insufficient to hold the whole of the island, the enemy was attempting to establish a fortress zone in the northeast corner, defended by a line running some fifty miles westward from Catania on the east coast into the mountains, then northward to meet the coast again near the town of Cefalù.

Cockin explained that while American forces were closing in on this enclave from the west, Eighth Army's major thrust had been stopped south of Catania by massed German armour. The 1st Canadian Division had therefore been ordered to break the deadlock by making a left hook which would threaten Catania from the northwest.

Valguarnera had, in fact, been the opening battle in this operation. Stabbing at the map with his finger, Cockin went on to explain the form.

"We must swing eastward now, you see. But first we have to crack the hinge of Jerry's defence line on the other side of the Dittaino. Here."

The broad Dittaino River valley, five miles north of our bivouac, lay at the foot of a formidable range of barren mountains which reared toward the distant, snow-capped cone of volcanic Etna. Protruding from this ascending range, and lying directly in our path like some titanic, anchored battleship, an outlying bastion of the ascending mountains towered some three thousand feet above the valley, dominating the entire countryside for miles around. This was the "hinge."

Cockin pointed on the map to a small village named Assoro which seemed to be poised on the very lip of the sky-raking promontory.

"Very tough nut, I do believe," he said in his clipped, professorial style. "Key to the whole position though... First fortified by the Sicels about a thousand years BC. Been a citadel against invasion ever since... Old Roger the Norman built a cracking great castle there when he conquered Sicily... supposed to have been impregnable in his time... Shouldn't wonder, eh? Need a goat with wings to scale that bloody thing!"

"Any idea who's holding it?"

"Corps Intelligence thinks 15th Panzer-Grenadier Division's on our front. Part of old Rommel's crowd, y'know. Tough bunch of buggers, but tough or not, somebody's got to turf 'em out. Could well be us. Let's hope so, eh?"

I felt carefree, even exhilarated, as I made my way back to the olive grove where the company was bivouacked, for I had not yet acquired the old soldier's trick of automatically calculating the risks of a new operation—of weighing the odds. I was still naive enough to share Cockin's hope that Assoro might be ours to take.

When I woke next morning the sun had barely cleared the distant peaks but my groundsheet, spread over a pile of straw to make a mattress, was already hot to the touch. Someone was shaking my arm. I rolled over muzzily and found Al Park's long face hanging over me.

"Up and at 'em, sonny boy! Alex's gone off to BHQ for an O-group. Looks like there's another job of work for willing hosses!"

DURING THE NIGHT the Loyal Edmonton Regiment had reached the Dittaino and established a bridgehead across it. Before dawn they were relieved by our sister unit, the Royal Canadian Regiment, and, as the sun rose, men of the RCR crouched in hurriedly dug slit trenches and stared up in awe at the mighty crag of Assoro.

The Germans on the promontory remained unperturbed. They had little reason to be concerned, for it was obvious that a frontal attack up the tortuous and twisting roadway that climbed laboriously from the valley floor would be suicidal. Nor, apparently, could Assoro be outflanked. The only possible approach from westward was guarded by the hillcrest town of Leonforte which occupied almost as strong a natural defence position as Assoro itself. To the east lay a waste of gullies and gorges of the kind we had faced at Valguarnera, but one that ended at the foot of a nearly vertical rock face which soared almost a thousand feet to terminate at the ancient Norman castle crowning Assoro's summit.

Assoro had been successfully defended four thousand years earlier by men armed only with bronze swords, slings and spears. According to Cockin, it had never been successfully stormed since. Now, in our time, it was held by some of the world's best soldiers, armed with the most modern weapons. Assoro appeared to be virtually impregnable.

So indeed it seemed to Brigadier Howard Graham, commander of 1st Brigade, who had been given the task of taking it. And so it must have seemed to Lieutenant Colonel Bruce Sutcliffe when he in his turn received the order to mount the actual attack.

Having told Jimmy Bird to have the battalion O-group waiting for his return, and accompanied only by Cockin, Sutcliffe set out in mid-morning of July 20 to make his reconnaissance. Reaching the Dittaino, the two men crossed the dry riverbed on foot and made their way to a forward observation post. This was no more than a shallow slit trench, barely sufficient to shelter the artillery observer who already occupied it. Sutcliffe and Cockin crouched in the open, map boards in front of them and binoculars levelled, the lenses winking in the sun as they anxiously scanned the mighty battlement looming ahead of them. They did not realize that they were being regarded in their turn.

On the Assoro scarp the crew of an Eighty-eight laid their gun over open sights. Seconds later a cloud of yellow dust and black smoke obscured the observation post in the valley below... and under its pall Sutcliffe lay dead and Cockin dying.

The loss of those who had been killed in the tumult and confusion of earlier actions had not yet been deeply perceived by us, but this new stroke of death was something else. It shredded the pale remnants of the illusion that real war was not much more than an exciting extension of battle games, and it fired us with rage against the enemy. This killing, before battle had been joined, seemed singularly vicious, almost obscene. When I heard news of it, I began to understand something of Alex Campbell's hatred of the Germans.

With Sutcliffe's death, command of the Regiment passed to Major Lord John Tweedsmuir. Barely thirty years of age, soft-spoken, kindly, with a slight tendency to stutter, he was a tall, fair-haired English romantic out of another age... his famous father's perhaps. "Tweedie," as we called him behind his back, had as a youth sought high adventure as a Hudson's Bay Company trader in the Arctic, then as a rancher on the African veldt, and finally as a soldier in a Canadian infantry battalion. But until this hour real adventure in the grand tradition had eluded him.

Going forward on his own reconnaissance that afternoon in company with the new second-in-command, Major "Ack Ack" Kennedy, Tweedsmuir looked up at the towering colossus of Assoro with the visionary eye of a Lawrence of Arabia, and saw that the only way to accomplish the impossible was to attempt the impossible. He thereupon decided that the battalion would make a right flank march by night across the intervening trackless gullies to the foot of the great cliff, scale that precipitous wall and, just at dawn, take the summit by surprise.

When Brigadier Graham, a Hasty Pee himself and Lieu-tenant Colonel Sutcliffe's predecessor as the Regiment's com-manding officer, heard the plan, his immediate reaction was to veto it. Years later he told me:

"It seemed like arrant madness. The likelihood that Tweedsmuir would lose the whole battalion seemed almost a dead certainty. I had a horrible vision of Balaklava and the Charge of the Light Brigade, and I was about to tell him: nothing doing! But then I thought, my God, he just *might* pull it off. So I let him go... but I sweat blood for the next twelve hours."

My own first knowledge of what was afoot came at our company O-group. Having given us the general plan, Alex trenchantly filled in the details.

"There's to be a special assault company of twenty picked men and one officer from each of the rifle companies, and I'm to command the lot. We'll carry nothing but weapons and ammunition. We'll lead the battalion cross-country, scale the cliff and take the castle. Then we'll hold it till the rest of the unit gets there. Ryan, you're senior subaltern so you'll stay back and take command of Able. Park, you'll help him out. Mowat, you'll come with me."

I never knew why Alex picked me. He must have been aware since early in my tenure with Seven Platoon that I was not the stuff of which heroes are made. Perhaps he wanted to give me an opportunity which, if I could manage to live up to it, would confer on me a tiny touch of what the French call *la gloire* and so turn me into a real fighting soldier. On the other hand, since we chosen officers were each to pick our own twenty men, he may have felt he *had* to take me in order to ensure that the best of Seven Platoon's unmannered but hard-fighting toughs joined the assault company.

In any event, the mere fact that I had been selected filled me with such overweening pride that, according to a disgruntled Park, I was as swollen with it "as a frog full of fart." But at the same time I was quivering with internal tremors, not so much at the prospects of what the enemy might do but at the thought of having to measure up to what would be required of me. Fortunately, there was not much time to worry. A scant two hours remained before we were due to move off from the start line.

There was barely time enough to select my men and see that they were briefed and armed for the task ahead. I included all the men of Mitchuk's section, for, with the exception of A.K. Long, they were the toughest of the tough. I hesitated about Long, but because I felt an inner kinship with him, he too joined our band.

By dusk we had sorted ourselves out, stripped for action, and eaten an enormous meal. As warriors we did not look particularly prepossessing. The large packs and kitbags which contained our spare clothing, boots, blankets and personal possessions had not, through some staff blunder, been offloaded on the invasion beaches. Consequently, after ten days with virtually no chance to repair or clean our clothing or ourselves, we were a dirty and ragged lot. Torn shorts and trousers did not matter much, but our socks were worn to shreds and were so matted and sweat-hardened that some men had discarded them. Worse still, our boots, subjected first to a soaking in salt water and then to many miles of marching on stony roads and rocky slopes, were cracked and gaping; a serious matter for a company of foot-sloggers engaged on a mission such as ours.

Tweedsmuir did what he could. Bren carriers were provided to transport us as far forward as possible. This was not very far. Having crossed the Dittaino on a rough diversion bulldozed by the engineers under enemy shellfire, the carriers were able to climb only a few hundred feet before being halted by a chaos of steep-sided gullies, knife-edged ridges and boulder-strewn *torrentes*—seasonal riverbeds, now dry as dust.

It was nearly 2100 hours and we were running late. Hurriedly we clambered off our iron steeds and formed up in single file. There was not a breath of wind and the air was filled with a pungent odour that nagged at my memory until I realized it was the tang of sage—a scent I had last smelled in the summer of 1938 on the arid plains of southwestern Saskatchewan where I had gone to study prairie dogs, sage hens, rattlesnakes and burrowing owls. That seemed an interminable distance in the past. Now I was part of a sinuous human centipede crawling on hundreds of awkward feet into the gathering darkness of another desert, in another world.

We did our best to be silent, for we were tensely fearful of discovery. It seemed inconceivable that the Germans would not at least have listening posts on this exposed flank, no matter how secure they felt.

There were some terrifying moments. The first came when our scouts stumbled on a man-made stone parapet that turned out to be a masked machine-gun post. It was unoccupied, but so recently had it been abandoned that crusts of dark bread left lying on the ground were still moist.

Hours later I was in the lead when I heard the rattle of stones on the far slope of a black gully into which we were blindly descending. I sank back into the shadows, tensed for the exploding moment. I heard rifles and Bren guns being softly cocked and held my own carbine before me at hip level, finger sweating on the trigger. There was indistinct movement and then a herd of goats slowly emerged into the dim starlight and, behind them, a ragged Sicilian youth. He did not see us at first but the goats did and snorted as he drove them forward. Then he was face to face with me, gaping incredulously as he took in the motionless shapes of armed men on every side. He said not a word but passed slowly on as in a dream.

As the night began to wane we were driven onward by increasing urgency, knowing we had to reach that massive cliff and scale it before the dawn revealed us to watchers who had the view of eagles. Fatigue was taking its toll but there could be no slowing down. The whispered order came forward, man to man, telling us to let the second assault platoon move into the lead so the pace could be maintained.

My twenty shadows and I slumped amongst the rocks while twenty others stumbled past. Many of them were limping. My own right foot was an agony because of a cracked sole through which gravel and twigs had worked their way. But I saw one man with no boots at all, stubbornly struggling through the mountains of Sicily on his bare, white feet.

As we fell in at the rear of the assault company, I yearned for one of those magical Benzedrine tablets which had sustained me on the long march from the beaches. I did not think I could hold out much longer.

Yet on we went—and on—until, at about 0400, under the pallid light of the late-rising crescent moon, we scaled the final ridge... and were appalled to find that the base of the mountain wall looming sheer above was still separated from us by a gully a hundred or so feet deep and as steep-sided as any ancient moat.

There was no way around it. Neither was there time to beat a retreat before dawn would catch us in the open. Somehow we lowered our aching bodies into that great ditch, struggled through the rubble of boulders that filled the bottom and finally stood, gasping, at the foot of the precipice of Assoro whose crest was still hidden in the fading night.

During the climb that followed, each of us performed his own private miracle. From ledge to ledge we oozed upward like some vast mould. Those who faltered clung with straining muscles until someone heaved from behind or hauled them from above. Weapons were passed up hand to hand; and no man dropped so much as a clip of ammunition... which was as well, for any sound by one would have been fatal to us all.

Alex had ordered my platoon and one other to lead the climb. My crowd was on the left and we were luckier than our companion platoon for we eventually reached some narrow terraces which may have been constructed in some distant age to grow food for beleaguered dwellers in the castle, but which had been abandoned to thorns and weeds for centuries past. These made progress a little easier, but by the time we had scrambled up over several of them I had reached the end of my tether. Someone heaved himself past me, turned and gave the thumbs-up signal. It was A.K. Long. He leapt up to the next ledge, then caught my hand and pulled me after him.

To the eastward a ripple of light was spreading across the sky. Dawn was bursting on us with subtropic swiftness. Long jumped to catch the lip of what seemed to be the next terrace and disappeared above me. Then with horrifying abruptness the silence was destroyed by the barking of a Tommy gun.

The voice of God Himself announcing the world's end could not have terrified me more. I was certain that the harsh staccato, reverberating back and forth from cliff to cliff, would assail the ears of every German within a hundred miles. With a convulsive effort I clawed at the rim of what proved to be the last ledge, and hauled myself over the top.

The crumbling wall of the ancient castle loomed close at hand. Directly in front of me and only a few feet distant, A.K. Long was down on one knee with his Tommy levelled at three German privates standing as rigid as store dummies beside a tripod-mounted telescope. Sprawled at their feet lay an artillery sergeant... the first man to die that day upon the crest of Mount Assoro.

A.K. Long glanced sideways at me and his expression was one of vast astonishment. When he spoke he sounded almost embarrassed, as if he felt he owed me or perhaps the surviving Germans some kind of an apology.

"The crazy bastard... went for his damn gun..."

His voice trailed off and in the ensuing silence we seemed fixed in a tableau of absolute immobility, puppets deprived of the will of a manipulator, unable to move a muscle of our own.

Then the moment shattered. All along the cliff edge steel-helmeted heads began to appear and men hauled themselves up onto the few acres of relatively flat ground which crowned the summit. George Baldwin, leader of another of the assault platoons, saw me and yelled that he would search the castle ruins. I waved agreement, and as soon as the rest of my platoon had crowded up behind me, I led them at a run across the plateau and a few yards down the opposite slope to the shelter of some low, stone walls. Sure that the firing must have alerted the Germans, I expected them to begin shelling us at any moment. But secure in their belief that Assoro was impregnable, they had posted no troops there other than the artillery observation team which Long had dealt with; and if any Germans elsewhere heard the one brief burst from A.K.'s gun, they misread its message.

It was full daylight now. Close below us were the huddled roofs of Assoro village, with skeins of blue smoke rising from the chimney pots. A quarter of a mile farther down the slope a narrow-gutted road ran south to the main German defence positions on the lip of the massif overlooking the valley of the Dittaino.

To our amazement, we beheld clusters of German soldiers strung out all along this road, gathered around their morning fires in a scene of cheerful, almost domestic tranquility. Through my binoculars I could see some of them shaving. Others stood, stripped to the waist, enjoying the first warmth of the sun. A dispatch rider puttered lazily along on his motorcycle, waving to some anti-aircraft gunners who were breakfasting from a steaming portable field kitchen. There was a rumble of heavy engines and the head of a supply convoy appeared out of the north. One, two, a dozen trucks hove slowly into view, gears grinding on the steep gradients as they brought forward their loads of rations, water and ammunition.

Lying beside me, Sergeant Bates was fairly wriggling with excitement.

"Shit a brick! Will you look at that! Let's clobber the sons a bitches quick!"

Before I could give an order, a Bren gunner in one of the other platoons tightened his trigger finger. Instantly the dozen Brens of the assault company went into action, reinforced by several 2-inch mortars and three score rifles.

This outpouring of fire from Assoro's crest must have come as a shattering surprise to the Germans down below; and had they been troops of a lesser calibre, a debacle such as had occurred at Valguarnera must have ensued. But the 15th Panzer-Grenadiers were old soldiers, toughened in Africa and of a fighting breed.

Although several trucks were hit and two or three burst into flames, the surviving drivers flung themselves into the ditches and began returning our fire with their machine pistols. The 20-mm anti-aircraft troop leapt to their guns, cranked down the barrels and were soon hosing us with streams of tracer high explosive. I even saw two cooks abandon their pots and pans to seize rifles and open fire upon us.

They were a courageous lot, but we had the advantages of surprise, good cover and overwhelming fire power, and one by one their weapons fell silent.

The alarm had swiftly reached the Germans manning the forward positions hidden from our view half a mile south of us. At once they began sending their front-line vehicles back up the road to prevent them from being cut off. Trucks and weapons carriers in groups of two or three came roaring along at full speed with rifles and machine pistols flaring up at us as they ran the gamut. Some got through, but before long the wreckage of those that failed had completely blocked the road. Thereupon, three armoured half-tracks veered off onto the verges and ground up the slopes toward us through a tangle of vineyards. Immune to our small-arms fire, they were only halted by the increasing steepness of the slope. Once stopped, medium machine-gun and 81-mm mortar teams leapt out of them, took cover and engaged us fiercely.

The battle was not yet half an hour old and already the Germans were counterattacking. Worse was soon to come. Several field and medium batteries located just to the north of us, covering the approaches to Leonforte, swivelled their guns to bear at almost point-blank range upon Assoro's peak.

At Valguarnera we had sown the wind. Now the whirlwind burst upon us.

I HAD JUST moved my platoon a little farther down the slope to a more protected position when the world exploded in an appalling cacophony of sound and fury. The cramped plateau onto which nearly five hundred men were now crowded virtually vanished under a mounting pall of dust and smoke, shot through with malevolent tongues of flame.

Dicky Bird, who had been left behind at rear Battalion Headquarters on the far side of the Dittaino, was anxiously observing Assoro.

"It looked absolutely ghastly! The whole top of the mountain seemed to blow up. I was sure I'd have to indent for a brand-new battalion. I didn't see how any of you poor sods could *possibly* survive."

Although most of the shells were falling to the north of my platoon position, the fury of that barrage was paralyzing. I lay flat on my belly behind a section of stone fence, scrabbling at the rock-hard ground with my tin hat in a frenzied attempt to burrow into the heart of the mountain. A consuming desire to become a mole was, I suspect, common to most of us as we endured this, our first heavy artillery bombardment.

But we were not moles and we could not escape. Neither could we retreat, as we had done at Valguarnera, since any attempt to descend the cliff would have invited massacre. We could not even relieve our situation by attacking, for our supplies of ammunition were already perilously low. Yet to stay where we were meant piecemeal destruction under the shattering weight of fire and steel which fell upon us.

The noise, smoke and confusion were so great that I was cut off from everyone, except Bates and a couple of men from Nine Platoon who were huddling behind the same broken wall that sheltered me. I did not know that several members of my assault platoon had already been wounded, nor that Sharon and Robinson, that steady and inseparable pair, had been obliterated by a direct hit on their shared slit trench. I only knew our situation was desperate and growing worse.

But desperation sharpens wits. At this juncture someone remembered the artillery spotter's telescope which A.K. Long had captured. And some brave soul dodged the shell bursts in order to retrieve the instrument and carry it to a partially ruined goat shed on the northern slope where Tweedsmuir and Kennedy had set up their command post. From this vantage point they could look northward into the valleys where the enemy artillery was sited. Having once been an artilleryman himself, Kennedy knew how to direct counter-battery fire. With the aid of the spotting-scope, whose vernier scales enabled him to calculate distances and angles, he began pinpointing the enemy gun positions. He was able to relay these back to our own artillery because, since our backpack radios had proved useless at Valguarnera, Tweedsmuir had insisted that our signallers bring along a massive, long-range set of a kind normally mounted in tanks. The signallers got this radio to the foot of the precipice on the back of a mule, which then collapsed and died of exhaustion. Hoisting it up the cliff must have been a near-Herculean task, but somehow they succeeded.

Slowly now the tide began to turn. As the enemy guns fired up at us, their muzzle flashes gave them away, and short minutes later salvos from our field and medium batteries came crashing down upon them. Kennedy kept up the counter-battery work until by noon many of the enemy guns were permanently out of action and the rest had withdrawn to safer sites out of range of Assoro's Cyclopean eye.

The initial bombardment having subsided to sporadic shelling, we collected our wounded—more than a score in number—and carried them to the shelter of a shallow cave where they were laid upon a common bed of straw. The narrow space soon looked and stank like a slaughterhouse. Blood was everywhere, glaring from torn, dust-whitened clothing, naked grey flesh and yellow straw. Captain Krakauer, our medical officer, had only first-aid kits with which to work and so could do little except try to staunch the gaping wounds. Yet there were no outcries of agony, perhaps because the blessed anesthesia of shock still dulled the pain. I found I had lost one man killed and three wounded from my hybrid platoon, but most of the other platoons had suffered heavier losses.

We survivors were slow to recover our wits. The several hundred shells which had fallen within the narrow confines of the battalion area with such violence had left us almost comatose. Action was the only effective antidote; but there was not a great deal to distract us once the casualties had been dealt with, except to deepen our shallow scrapes of foxholes in anticipation of a renewal of the fury. I was actually grateful when Alex sent his runner with a message ordering me to take a patrol into the village and see if it was free of Germans.

I decided to take only one man with me, and I chose A.K. Long. Any doubts I might earlier have had about his soldierly capabilities had vanished after his performance on the cliff.

With a casualness that amounted almost to negligence— a reaction to the intolerable impact of the bombardment we had just undergone—I led the way along a zigzag cobbled path descending steeply toward the clustering stone houses. Although bursts of small-arms fire were coming from some-where to the north of the village, the whistle and whine of passing bullets seemed almost harmless by comparison with what we had so recently endured.

We were crossing a stone footbridge over a deep ravine, walking upright and carelessly silhouetted against the skyline, when Long lurched against me, jerking me to my knees.

"What the hell...?"

"I'm hit!"

He crouched over, peering at his right thigh... and then began to chuckle.

A bullet had gone clean through the stock of his slung rifle and glanced off the brass fittings on his web belt, dealing him a bruising blow but not even breaking the skin.

"Born lucky, I guess," was his only comment.

We finished crossing the bridge at a run, bent dou-ble behind the protection of the parapet, and much more circumspectly now we entered a tangle of steep and narrow alleys. Everything around us bore testimony to the great antiquity and equally great poverty of the village. The squalid stone houses hunkering against the slope seemed rooted in windrows of filth which had built up since the last heavy rain and would continue to accumulate until a new deluge washed the offal and excrement down the reeking streets and tumbled it into the valley below. The townsfolk must all have gone to ground during the shelling, for the place seemed lifeless and abandoned except for black waves of flies that rose and eddied at our feet.

The emptiness of the streets made us uneasy. Cautiously we hugged the flaking walls until we came to a tiny square. As we crouched uncertainly beside a crumbling building, I saw an arm beckoning to me from a nearby doorway. A.K. covered me with his rifle as I slid sideways to investigate, carbine cocked and ready. Then the owner of the arm stepped out into the brilliant sunshine and I found myself being effusively greeted, in excellent English, by a tall Italian captain.

Full of camaraderie and goodwill, he explained that he and his company had been hiding in nearby cellars since dawn—hiding not from us but from their German allies. His story was that he and his men had been sent forward during the night to take over a part of the German-held front, but that they had deliberately lost themselves.

"We are finished with this war. It is the Germans' business, so let the Germans have it. Barbarians that they are! Now we happily surrender to you Britishers who are our liberators."

"Canadians, actually," I replied as I somewhat reluctantly accepted the automatic pistol he extended, butt first, toward me. I did not think the addition of forty or fifty Italian prisoners to our beleaguered garrison on the summit would prove much of an advantage to us.

"It's pretty hot up where we are," I suggested. "Might be better if you fellows stayed down here until things cool off."

The tall *capitano* smiled and nodded agreeably.

"Just how close *are* the Germans anyway?" I asked.

He continued to smile as he pointed down one of the mean little streets leading out of the square.

"They are there," he said cheerfully. "In the *casas* at the bottom of that *strada*. They just came up. Many of them. Very well armed. Perhaps you should bring down a few more of your men?"

"Jesus!" I gulped. "Perhaps I should! *Grazia, grazia...* Come on, Long, let's vamoose!"

We made a precipitate withdrawal, arriving back rather breathless at Company Headquarters, which Alex had established in a break in the castle walls.

Alex was not surprised by my report. He told me that a Baker Company platoon attempting to descend toward the road at the northern outskirts of the village had just been driven back by heavy small-arms fire. The Germans were closing the ring around us.

I had scarcely rejoined the platoon when the day was rent by a rasping, metallic screeching that rose to an ear-splitting pitch and volume, culminating in a series of stupendous explosions that shook the solid rock beneath my cringing flesh. A blast of furnace-hot air buffeted me, and six coiling plumes of smoke and dust sprang, towering, above the castle ruins.

This was our introduction to the chief horror of the front-line soldier's life in World War ii, the rocket artillery which the Germans had misleadingly code-named Nebelwerfer—smoke thrower—and which the Eighth Army, encountering it during the last stages of the North Africa campaign, christened Moaning Minnie.

There were two varieties of these frightful things. The largest contained a bursting charge of 110 pounds of TNT. A smaller version held a charge of only 40 pounds, but was fired in salvos of five or six at a time. These projectiles needed no guns to speed them on their way. They were fired electrically from simple angle-iron or even wooden frames, or from clusters of "stovepipe" tubes mounted on two wheels. They could readily be concealed in any ditch or behind any wall or shack, and our counter-battery fire was of little avail against them since the Germans seldom fired twice from the same position.

The Moaning Minnie bombardment which followed was well-nigh unendurable. Although I had experienced spasms of fear during the previous few days, what I felt now was undiluted terror. As salvo after salvo screamed into our positions and the massive explosions and shuddering blast waves poured over me, my whole body grew rigid, muscles knotting so tightly they would no longer obey my orders.

Mercifully this new bombardment did not last long. Unable to bring transport forward because of Kennedy's observation of the approach roads and the devastatingly accurate fire of our guns, the Germans were having difficulty replenishing their ammunition and so had to practise some economy. On the other hand, as we had begun the day with only the ammunition we could carry on our backs up Assoro's precipice, we were now literally reduced to counting every round. We had virtually no food; and what muddy water we could obtain from a shallow well near the castle barely sufficed to meet the needs of the increasing numbers of wounded, let alone the rest of us lying, parched and baking, on that shard of rock under the pitiless Sicilian sky.

By mid-afternoon an uneasy lull lay over Assoro. There was still some sporadic shelling, and when I made a visit to Battalion Headquarters on Alex's behalf, I had to run a gamut of machine-gun fire. By then the Germans had occupied the whole of Assoro village and had sprinkled it with snipers who kept us under a desultory but dangerous fire from broken windows and from holes punched in walls and roofs. It was one of these unseen sharpshooters who, for the first time, made me feel real hatred for the soldiers who opposed us.

My platoon's job was to guard the southeastern approaches to the summit, but there was so little enemy activity below our segment of the perimeter that I had allowed all my men, except for a few sentries, to take advantage of the lull and try to get some sleep. I too was dozing when a sentry called out to me. I crawled to the edge of the walled terrace where he was lying and cautiously peered over it, mindful of the snipers in the houses off to our right.

A couple of hundred feet below, a grey and obviously aged little donkey was laboriously picking his way through a thicket of vineyard poles in the direction of the village. He was carrying two wickerwork panniers slung on his back.

"Where'd he come from?" I asked the sentry.

"Don't know, sir. One minute there was nothing on the hill, the next he was just there. What do we do about it? Might be some grub in his baskets."

"Do nothing," I said. "Too risky to try and reach him. Leave him be."

There being nothing else of interest to see, I was about to crawl back to my slit trench when the sentry exclaimed:

"Goddamn!... the donk's been hit."

Something—a stray bullet was my guess—had struck the little beast in the haunch. It had hit him hard, for although he did not seem to realize he was wounded and continued struggling on through the vineyard, his left hind leg dangled slack and useless.

I had barely taken this in when a sharp crack from somewhere in the village signalled a shot from a sniper's rifle. At almost the same instant I heard the meaty *thunk* as a bullet struck the donkey's other hind leg close to the knee, shattering bone and flesh with such an impact that the little animal was flung over on its side. It lay there, seemingly stunned, but in a minute or two it began struggling to get back on its feet.

I realized then that the first hit had been no stray bullet. A German sniper was deliberately shooting at the beast, aiming to disable it, either to entertain himself or to demonstrate his marksmanship. A third shot cracked out. The donkey, which had somehow managed to lever itself up onto its front legs, collapsed again—with a third leg shattered! It was now completely immobilized, except for its lop-eared, grey-muzzled head which lifted... sagged to the ground... lifted... sagged again... lifted...

The soldier lying beside me, himself a farmer, could not contain himself.

"That rotten, fucking Kraut! I'd like to blow his fucking balls off!"

Two or three silent minutes passed, and still that stubborn old head rose up... and fell again. I could no longer stand it.

"For God's sake, kill the poor bloody thing!"

I was talking to the unknown, unseen German, but the sentry beside me took the meaning. Quickly he raised his rifle, aimed and fired. The old donkey moved no more.

The lull drew on into the late afternoon. Both sides were waiting for night: we for the hoped-for arrival of reinforcements and supplies; the Germans so they could mount a counterattack in darkness.

An hour after sunset we came under another thundering bombardment and, as it ended, a battalion of Panzer-Grenadiers attacked from the northwest. They were met, halted and broken mainly by the massed fire of three regiments of our distant guns, called down upon them by Kennedy and that blessed radio set. Twice more the Grenadiers tried to clamber up the slopes. Twice more they were driven back. After the last attempt they retreated to the road. Shortly thereafter we heard an upsurge of vehicle noises. The Germans had given up Assoro, and were pulling out from their positions overlooking the Dittaino.

AS THE MORNING sun glared down upon us, the sounds of war became muted in the distance. Along the wreckage-strewn road below the village our own Bren carriers appeared, grinding up toward us. Around the precious well men washed the dust and grime out of their eyes. We could stand down now and take our rest. But a mile or so to the north of us the crew of a Nebelwerfer, preparing to abandon their position, fired a projectile in a last defiant gesture.

A banshee screech echoed over the brown hills, then the rocket plunged screaming out of the pale sky and hit the stone curbing of the well. When the black, acrid smoke cleared, it was to reveal the mangled bits and pieces of four dead men. It was a bitter way to learn that battles end but war goes on.

The stretcher-bearers, helped by some of the Italian soldiers who had now emerged from their shelters in the town, were trying to gather up the victims of this carnage as I passed by, responding to a message ordering me to report to headquarters with all my kit and accompanied by my batman.

I had no idea what this presaged, and did not much care. I had been suffering from dysentery during the past two days and in the night it had become so much worse that my guts were writhing. Weak and sweating I followed Doc Macdonald to a villa below Assoro where Dicky Bird had set up his orderly room. He greeted me with a disapproving glance.

"My goodness, Squib, you *do* look dreadful. But you're to be 1o again and the co wants to see you, so for Heaven's sake, get yourself cleaned up!"

I was willing but the flesh was weak. As Doc was trying to ease me out of my stained and stinking clothes, I fainted. When I came to, the medical officer was standing beside the liberated mattress on which I lay.

"You've got it bad," Krakauer said judiciously. "Might be amoebic—there's blood enough. Anyhow, it's back down the line for you."

WITHIN AN HOUR of again becoming battalion intelligence officer, I found myself in a jeep ambulance bouncing south. With me went Regimental Sergeant-Major Angus Duffy and a corporal from Baker Company, both in the same fix as myself. The corporal raged against his fate—and against the medical officer.

"That son of a Brighton bitch!" he cursed. "After I shit my way across half of Sicily, doing my job as good as any fucker in the outfit, and *just* when our platoon sergeant buys it and I'm up to get his stripe, that bastard tells me I got to be evacuated! *Evacuated!* I'm so goddamn evacuated I'm like to float away like a free balloon!"

Almost as soon as we reached the casualty clearing station we were shipped out again, this time in a real ambulance. At dusk we arrived at a British field hospital. It was housed in a decrepit monastery and was chaotically overcrowded. Duffy and I were given canvas stretchers in lieu of beds, while the corporal was taken to some distant ward. We lay in a broad, stone-flagged hallway so congested that there was scarcely room to move between the stretchers. Most of the casualties were freshly wounded men from a British armoured division which had been savaged by a German counterattack near Catania. Many were fearfully burned and still in shock. All of them were very quiet.

I ought to have felt like a slacker, lying in such company, but I was too sick to care, so weak I could not even shuffle to the latrine. Duffy gave me what help he could. Sick as he was himself, he was still the regimental sergeant-major and, as such, determined to look after "his" men even in hospital.

It was a night to be forgotten. Next day was no better; but during the morning of July 25 I sank into an exhausted sleep— only to be awakened a few hours later by Duffy standing fully dressed beside my stretcher with my clothing over his arm and my boots in his hand.

"You'd best get up. There's been a balls-up at the front. Five loads of our lads have already come in and there's more on the way. An ambulance is going right back up. We should be on it."

If it had been anyone else, I would have resisted, for I had no inclination to leave the hospital, unpleasant as it was. It was not that I felt myself physically incapable of returning to battle—the truth was that I did not ever again want to have to taste the terror which had overwhelmed me at Assoro. The desire for action which had been my ruling passion since enlistment had collapsed like a pricked balloon—to be replaced by a swelling sense of dread. However, a regimental sergeant-major is next to God in an infantry outfit and so, twenty minutes later, Duffy and I were aboard the northbound ambulance. We did not even take time to get ourselves discharged from the hospital.

All that hot afternoon we made our slow way through dense military traffic and in the evening we rejoined our regiment and found it shaken and bloodied in defeat.

A white-faced Dicky Bird almost wept with relief at seeing Duffy.

"The colonel's wounded and gone down the line," he lamented. "Kennedy's hit and half delirious. There's *nobody* left to clean up the mess!" He paused to run his hands through his hair and down over his face as if trying to sweep away some shadow we could not see. "Oh my God, Squib, it was a massacre!"

"All right now, sir," Duffy spoke soothingly as to a child. "I'll get on with it."

He swung briskly out the door, and I followed him in search of Seven Platoon. I found the twenty or so survivors huddled about a tea fire in a nearby field; and as Corporal Hill described what had happened, I found myself silently thanking whatever gods there be for having kept me out of it.

"It was a bloody schlemozzle right from the start. The RCRS were sent off down the road from Assoro with a squadron of tanks and ran smack into an ambush in some hills just beyond the next village—place called Nissoria. They lost a hell of a lot of men and a bunch of tanks, and any goddamn fool should have known after that those hills were held in strength, but we were ordered right on in there anyway. No reconnaissance, no artillery fire to soften things up, no tanks, no *nothing*—and it was pitch-dark by then. Supposed to be a surprise attack! Jesus H. Christ, it was that all right—a fucking big surprise for us...

"Jerry let the forward companies, us and Charley, get half-way up the slopes, then he lit the place up with star shells like it was Maple Leaf Gardens on a Saturday night, and started to pour the shit onto us from all directions. It was blood and guts from then on in! Tweedsmuir must've got hit pretty near right away, then Kennedy stopped one and by then nobody knew what the hell was happening. It was every man for himself. Some crawled back on their bellies. Some guys were too scared to move and Jerry picked 'em up and put 'em in the bag next morning. Some was dead, and some so shot-up they couldn't move...

"A.K. Long was one of them. A mortar bomb smashed both his legs and filled his guts with shrapnel. He was no more'n a hop and a skip away from me, and when it began to get light I could see him sitting with his back to a banged-up tree, looking as calm as if he was on a village green in England. I was flat on my belly with three or four others, trying to figure how the hell we were going to get out of there, and I figured we had to at least *try* and get A.K. out too.

"He wasn't having any. I told him to try and crawl across to us. He just shook his head and took out that goddamn old pipe of his and lit her up. And then, by Jesus, he hauls out some book or other and starts to read . . .

"You couldn't believe it! All that shit flying about and him sitting there reading a goddamn book! Finally he calls over at me: 'Get out of here, Hill. The Jerry medics will look after me.' Just then somebody laid down some smoke and it was our only chance so we got cracking fast . . . Old A.K. Long! He was a right good son of a bitch."

LEAVING SEVEN PLATOON in order to return to the intelligence officer's job was a considerable wrench. The two months I had spent with the platoon seemed like a lifetime. Although I knew very little of the past lives and inner beings of those thirty men, I had been more firmly bound to them than many a man is to his own blood brothers, and yet, sadly, it was not a lasting tie. I would not have believed it possible, but I was to discover that once I had left them they would become almost as irrelevant to my continuing existence as if I had known them only in some distant moment of illusion.

This was a disturbing discovery and for a time I thought it must indicate a singular lack of emotional depth in me. I was deluded by the conventional wisdom which maintains that it is personal linkages that give a group its unity. I was slow to comprehend the truth: that comrades-in-arms unconsciously create from their particulate selves an imponderable entity which goes its own way and has its own existence, regardless of the comings and goings of the individuals who are its constituent parts. Individuals are of no more import to it than they were in the days of our beginnings when the band, the tribe, was the vehicle of human survival. Once out of it, it ceases to exist for you—and you for it.

For a time after again becoming intelligence officer, I continued to visit Seven Platoon, but these visits became less and less frequent and eventually ceased altogether as I realized that my only remaining ties were memories of that brief period when I had, in truth, *belonged*. I did not belong anymore.

ON JULY 27 we watched 2nd Brigade go forward to a full-scale attack on Nissoria, with two battalions making the actual assault, assisted by massive artillery and tank support and even by Desert Air Force fighter-bombers. Somebody back there had belatedly learned a lesson. We were not bitter about our own experience, only greatly relieved that we had been spared from taking part in this new attack, for the Regiment had now suffered over two hundred casualties since the landing—a loss of more than a quarter of its fighting strength.

We were well content to rest for a few days. One afternoon the terrible heat was relieved by a spectacular cloudburst that began with hail, then turned to a fall of solid water. The parched ground steamed and smoked. Dry gorges and *torrentes* became wild, roaring rivers. Soaked to the skin we stood in our bivouac area entranced by this benison, or we ran about shedding our grubby clothes in ecstasy. This was happiness, and it was doubled next day when our packs and kitbags finally caught up with us. At last we had the luxuries of clean clothing, new boots, even a few hoarded candy bars, together with such fragile physical links with another world as packets of old letters, a few books, some photographs.

Clean, freshly clad and shod, we were in an ebullient mood when on August 1 we moved eastward to take part in another battle.

The objective this time was the town of Regalbuto in the rough hill country below Mount Etna where the Germans were making a stubborn stand. Regalbuto was defended by troops of the Hermann Göring Division, who had fought a British brigade and our two sister regiments, the RCR and the 48th Highlanders, to a bloody standstill on the approaches to the town. We were ordered in to break the stalemate.

Major Kennedy, who had refused to be evacuated after being hit in the leg at Nissoria, now succeeded Tweedsmuir, whose wounds were severe enough to send him to hospital in North Africa. Kennedy was especially determined that this, his first battle as commanding officer, would be successful. I accompanied him to the Brigade O-group, and his first order thereafter was to me.

"What I want from you, Mowat, is dead simple. First find out every damn thing there is to know about Jerry's dispositions, then find a secure route around behind him that we can use to sneak in and knife him under his armpit."

Simple, was it?

I hurried off to visit my opposite number with the RCR who took me to his observation post on a hill overlooking Regalbuto. There we spent a most uncomfortable hour being mortared by an alert enemy while we tried to figure out just where the German positions were. After that I briefed a fighting patrol of twenty men, led by my friend George Baldwin, instructing them to find a concealed route around or through the German positions. Finally I put together all the intelligence information I could collect from 1st Brigade and from the flanking British brigade. Then, rather proud of myself, I reported to Kennedy.

"That *all* you've got?" he said impatiently when I had finished. "Take a motorbike and recce the highway into the goddamn town. Find out if we can send tanks that way!"

Crestfallen I cranked up the Intelligence Section's Norton and headed down the empty, dusty road toward Regalbuto. I had not gone far when it became apparent this was no road for tanks or for me either. It was defended by a troop of Eighty-eights who, for want of a more worthy target, began sniping at me and my motorcycle with high-explosive shells. Dishevelled and somewhat incoherent I reported back to Kennedy. He was unsympathetic.

"Hell's bells! If the road's no good, take a couple of carriers and find a route for tracked vehicles cross-country to the south!"

"But, sir," I protested, "it's already dusk and according to the maps there's no way *any* vehicle can get through there even in daylight."

"No way? *No way?* Goddamn it, boy, find a way!"

Smarting considerably, and no longer at all sure I wanted to be 10, I set off with two carriers into what seemed like an impassable chaos of cliffs and canyons.

Although the carrier men were skilled drivers, what we really needed were miracle workers. By midnight we had slogged the machines less than a mile, when one of them threw a track while the other bellied itself on the lip of a fifty-foot canyon. We were still stranded there when, an hour before dawn, we were overtaken by the rifle companies marching up to the attack in single file, with Kennedy limping at their head. I fully expected him to strip me of my remaining hide;

instead of which he merely grinned at me and my immobilized steel steeds.

"No good, eh? Well, I thought as much... but then you never know until you try."

THE BATTLE THAT followed was a classic example of how an action at the regimental level *should* be fought. Baldwin had made his undetected way through the German advance posts and had sent guides back for us. Shortly before dawn we had sneaked two companies into position on a commanding hill well inside the enemy defence perimeter. From the crest Kennedy and I and an accompanying artillery officer could see almost every move the still-unsuspecting Germans made, and stood ready to bring shellfire down as needed.

Zero hour came and, covered by Able and Dog companies and supported by our 25-pounder guns, Baker and Charley loped rapidly across an intervening valley and swarmed up the slopes of a long ridge behind Regalbuto almost before the enemy knew an attack was underway. There was some fierce hand-to-hand fighting, but we cleared the Germans off the ridge in less than an hour. The main enemy forces hurriedly withdrew to avoid being cut off, suffering heavy casualties as they departed. Regalbuto was ours and the way to the east lay open.

Word of our success must have been slower than usual in percolating back to high command. Next morning as we lounged on the slopes overlooking Regalbuto, we were visited by a squadron of U.S. Air Force medium bombers. In leisurely style they proceeded to churn the already battered streets and houses into heaps of smoking rubble.

Bruce Richmond, my intelligence sergeant, had been sitting beside me when the bombers came in. After their departure he struggled out of the ditch into which he had hastily flung himself and I heard for the first time that now-hackneyed phrase:

"Jesus H. Christ! With friends like *that,* who needs bloody enemies?"

HARRIED BY THE U.S. Fifth Army moving steadily eastward along the northern coast, and by the bulk of Eighth Army which, having been freed from the impasse in front of Catania by 1st Canadian Division's flanking thrust through the interior, was racing up from the south, the Germans and their reluctant Italian allies were now penned into a shrinking enclave in the extreme northeast corner of the island. It was apparent that the campaign was ending. After a few days in reserve near Regalbuto, the welcome word reached us that we were to be withdrawn from action.

However, before leaving the highlands under the loom of Etna's cone, there was something I had to do.

One blazing morning I borrowed the commanding officer's jeep and, accompanied by Corporal Hill, set out westward along the road to Nissoria.

We bounced along over broken pavement whose surface had been pulverized first by German trucks, tanks and guns, and then by ours. The things I saw were all familiar enough— scorched hill slopes, desiccated olive groves, clumps of whitewashed farm buildings; and the ubiquitous spoor of an advancing army... long lines of vehicles grumbling toward the front, untidy hillocks of supplies in roadside dumps, batteries of guns deployed in dusty fields—but the point of view seemed oddly different. It was a while before I realized why. For the first time since landing in Sicily, I was no longer being swept forward on the cresting wave of battle but was going backward into a past that, measured by ordinary temporal scales, was only yesterday but which, in view of the plethora of experiences and happenings it had embraced, had already metamorphosed into ancient history.

I was going back to look at a battlefield from which the living had passed on. Hill and I were making this journey to try and answer for ourselves the nagging question of what had finally happened to A.K. Long.

Our first stop was at a temporary graveyard where the Canadians who had been killed outright at Nissoria lay until such time as their bodies could be moved to some permanent resting place. It was a rough enough imitation of a cemetery—a cactus-strewn wasteland with forty or fifty mounds of reddish dirt clustered together and marked by small, white "issue" crosses, to each of which was nailed one of the paired identification tags we all wore around our necks. The transient bodies were shallowly buried and the heat was oppressive. The ripe stench of decay filled our nostrils as we worked our way up and down the lines of crosses, bending over to read the names stamped into the fibreboard discs. There were several Hasty Pees but Long was not among them.

"Perhaps the Jerries did pick him up after all?" I suggested.

"Maybe. And maybe the grave detail just never found him. But I know where he was."

Together we made our way up the long, barren slope where barely a week earlier Seven Platoon had made *its* way. The rising ground was almost as devoid of cover or shelter as a paved parking lot, and I shivered at the thought of what it must have been like when the star shells turned night into day and the enfilading machine guns opened up.

The evidence of what had happened was all around. Behind a pumpkin-sized bush lay a ripped bush shirt and an unravelled shell dressing, both black with dried blood that nevertheless still drew a few flies. Scattered about like debris flung from the crash of an airliner were steel helmets, occasional rifles, split bandoliers out of which spilled clips of .303 ammunition whose brass casings and silvered bullets glittered jewel-like under the white-hot sun. There were bits and pieces of web equipment, a carton of 2-inch mortar bombs, fragments of clothing fluttering in a hot wind beside the shallow, blackened craters which shells had blown in the flint-hard ground and scraps of paper everywhere. I puzzled over that. It looked almost as if some youthful and light-hearted paper chase had taken place. A blue airgraph letter form (so precious that only one was issued to each soldier every week) crinkled underfoot. It was as blank as the mind of the dead man who had left it there.

Then I recalled Pat Amoore and I searching the German dead near Valguarnera, casually tossing aside the unwanted contents of dead men's pockets and wallets—old letters, postcards, photographs. The Germans at Nissoria, searching the field after the fighting ended, had left us a similar legacy of torn and tattered memories tossed to the winds of time.

We came at last to the gully (it was a mere fold in the ground) where Hill and the survivors of his section had lain through interminable hours. He pointed out the tree—gnarled and twisted, not much more than a shrub—and we went over to it. Somehow I expected—hoped—to find the book A.K. had been reading, but it was not there. There was nothing of him to be found. The ground where he had fallen was the home of milling colonies of ants, and the blood he had spilled here had already undergone its permutation. There was nothing to be seen except for a swift brown lizard that darted up the shrapnel-lacerated bole of the tree and vanished amongst the few remaining grey and silver leaves.

"Not a goddamn trace!" Hill was perplexed. "Could be you're right. Jerry might have picked him up. One damn thing I know for sure, he was hit too bad to live for long... barring a miracle."

Neither of us believed in miracles. For the first time during the Sicilian campaign I experienced heartfelt pain at the loss of a comrade... which was passing strange, for I had never been his chum, had never really known the man. An enigma, he had lived among us for a while, then vanished from us... but I had felt for him... would feel for him in the years ahead.

Months later the Regiment was notified of the finding of a grave near a onetime German military hospital at Messina. Nailed to a Gothic cross above it was A.K. Long's dog tag.

The sullen heat of noon beat down on Hill and me as we made our way slowly toward the front in a stream of dusty traffic. By the time we reached the bivouac area, orders for us to move out of the line had already arrived.

Our war in Sicily was at an end.

PART III

And Death fell with me, like a deepening moan.

And He, picking a manner of worm, which half had hid

Its bruises in the earth, but crawled no further,

Showed me its feet, the feet of many men,

And the fresh-severed head of it, my head.

WILFRED OWEN · "THE SHOW"

THE ORDER READ: "1ST DIVISION will now proceed to a rest area, where the troops will enjoy a period of relaxation and the rewards for a job well done."

One hellishly hot morning in early August we loaded ourselves aboard a convoy of open trucks and set off on a hundred-mile trek to the southward. Late in the evening we arrived, dust-choked and dehydrated, at our destination a few miles from Grammichele, the scene of our first real action short weeks earlier.

One look at the rest area was enough to give us pause. While the base troops, headquarters staffs, supply services and those who seldom if ever heard a shot fired in anger took over comfortable billets in the coastal cities of Catania and Syracuse or in resort hotels at regal Taormina, the fighting soldiers of 1st Canadian Division found themselves banished to the desolate and dreary interior of the island.

Our portion turned out to be a scorched and stony plateau which distantly, and tantalizingly, overlooked the green plains of Catania and from whose arid heights we could, with binoculars, just glimpse the far blue waters of the Mediterranean.

Here, under an implacable sun, amongst scant thickets of bamboo and clumps of cactus, we were fated to remain for the balance of the month to enjoy our relaxation and rewards.

It was not a matter of choice. Under pain of summary punishment, we were confined to the Brigade area. No leaves of any sort were granted. All towns and cities (even dusty little Grammichele which we ourselves had captured) were placed strictly out of bounds. We were forbidden to fraternize with Italian civilians. We were forbidden to supplement our issue rations either by barter or purchase. We were not even permitted to buy vino, and were expected to rest content with an issue of one bottle of beer per man per week, and one bottle of whisky per officer per month.

As if this was not bad enough, hardly had we settled into the bivouacs which we built ourselves out of bamboo, groundsheets and straw, when we were set upon by a horde of tormentors.

Possibly in an attempt to justify their existence, non-combatant officers of every rank began to arrive in a steady stream of jeeps and staff cars, and subjected us to interminable pointless persecutions including detailed inspections of everything from carburetors to foreskins. When these busybodies grew fatigued from examining our latrines, cookhouses, underwear, first-aid kits, etcetera, they demanded ceremonial troop inspections which required long hours of preparation followed by equally long hours in parade formations under a blinding sun, while we waited for some VIP to make his brief appearance.

During a single week we were subjected to three such purgatories: once by General Montgomery, once by our divisional commander, and once by General McNaughton, commander-in-chief of the Canadian Army. Each took the opportunity to thank us on behalf of King and Country for our achievements. But concrete demonstrations of gratitude were notable by their absence, both in our blistering purgatory in Sicily and at home in Canada.

Although we were very short of reinforcements, the news from home told of a continuing evasion of overseas conscription by Mackenzie King's Liberal government; of anti-war riots led by Fascist sympathizers; of strikes by war workers for higher pay; and of the sacrifices being less than stoically endured by the civilian population which was having to submit to the horrors of sugar rationing.

It seemed to us that instead of being rewarded for our victories, we were being forced to do penance. Nor was this simple paranoia. Division passed down to Brigade, which passed down to us a training syllabus for the rest period, which had us up and hopping at 0600 hours and which was effective six days a week. On the seventh there was compulsory church parade, after which we were free to clean our kit and weapons.

Apart from being exhausting, the training was often asinine. I remember with almost undiminished anger a patrol exercise in which every man and officer in the Regiment had to engage, and which required that we who had clawed and fought our way across half of Sicily should spend twenty-four continuous hours clawing through the selfsame mountains once again.

When we finally had our first pay parade, we were given specially printed military *lire* which were virtually worthless since we were denied the opportunity to spend them. They were used mainly in surreptitious games of poker, though all forms of gambling were *also* forbidden and could only be enjoyed under the blind eye of an obliging superior.

The brass-hatted Mother Grundys of the staff, who so rigorously sought to deprive us of the pleasures fighting troops at rest might legitimately hope to enjoy, provided their own substitutes. They organized sports days for us (ah, the joys of the hundred-yard dash!); twice we were taken in tightly guarded convoys to swim in the sea; and to top it all off, on one momentous occasion we were entertained for two hours by a military band.

To add wormwood and gall, we knew our situation was unique among the fighting soldiers in Sicily. Only the Canadian Forces were treated like inmates of a reform school. The German army encouraged its troops to find whatever joy was to be had, even providing mobile brothels when local amenities proved inadequate. British and American troops spent generous leaves in Sicilian cities and coastal resorts, were free to scour the countryside for local food and drink and were, in general, encouraged to make the most of any respite from the miserable business of killing and being killed.

In the circumstances, it was inevitable that we would begin to feel a festering contempt for the pompous paper-pushers of our behind-the-lines bureaucracy, whose only discernible reason for existence seemed to be to make our lives a trial.

One such was a pasty-faced, pot-bellied major from some arcane financial section who appeared every time we withdrew into reserve, but never came near when we were within artillery range of the enemy. He pursued us with dogged tenacity through Sicily and Italy for six months, demanding that we rectify a discrepancy in the officers' mess accounts amounting to the horrendous sum of three pounds, nine shillings and six pence. He would not accept my explanation (I was mess secretary during much of this period) that my predecessor had been blown to bits together with the account books and the mess funds themselves when a landmine went off beneath his truck.

"That just won't do—won't do at all," the major huffed.

"He should have been blown up by a two-ton bomb instead?" I asked innocently.

The major glared angrily. "There should have been *copies* of the mess accounts kept in a safe place. The missing monies *must* be accounted for or you will be held personally answerable to the auditor-general!"

He demanded that I institute a full-scale Court of Inquiry to trace the missing funds. What I actually did was lead him on a merry chase for months, until I got so sick of his face that I collected the equivalent of the missing sum in captured German marks and sent it off to him. In due course I received his official receipt, properly stamped and signed, in quintuplicate.

PAT AMOORE and I were more successful in enjoying the rest period than most of our peers because as intelligence officers we had more freedom of action, as one of my letters home attests.

Pat and I have teamed up and built ourselves a sun-proof bamboo hut that only lacks a couple of houris to complete its comforts. Alas, there being no houris, we have to settle for a brace of large, copper-coloured lizards who seem to think the shack is theirs. They whistle at us in the night and drop cock-roaches in our ears... Pat savvies Italiano like a native so we do pretty well. We get most of our meals ourselves, or rather old Doc does. Gourmet cooking is just one of his many talents. Breakfast is cantaloupe, watermelon, grapes, and sometimes a pomegranate. Lunch and dinner feature fried eggplant and tomatoes, various pastas and goat cheese...

We get most of this stuff by exchange whereby the Eye-ties get our bully, margarine, hardtack and other inedibles, which they seem to relish, though maybe they feed it to their mules. Last week we had a suckling pig which cost two pair of issue boots and one rather holey blanket. For a pack of issue Victory cigs, the kind made in India of camel dung, troops-for-the-use-of, we get a basket full of cactus apples, green figs and tangerines. All totally illegal of course, which makes it twice as good...

Booze poses rather more of a problem. Yesterday Pat and I took off in a jeep ostensibly to do a recce for night patrol exercises, but instead hied ourselves out of 1st Div terri-tory to U.S. army turf. Specifically the town of Caltagirone which was lousy with Yanks wandering about chasing booze and skirts. Pat, who is a smoothie and really knows his way around, took us straight to the carabiniere (the local police). A couple of packs of cigs got us a uniformed cop who took us on the rounds of the best bootleggers. We trundled back to our Boy Scout Camp late at night with thirty litres of vino, some cognac, muscatel and liquid dynamite called grappa...

The Boss, Ack Ack Kennedy, was a bit brassed off when he heard what we'd been up to but he mellowed mightily when he saw the loot. The High-Priced Help would have our scalps if they but knew the things we do...

If there was little else in the way of relaxation, there was at least time for me to indulge in some exotic nature study:

> Birds are scarce and wary since anything that flies is meat to the Eyetie stewpots, but lizards and snakes abound as do tarantulas, scorpions and other strange invertebrates. I bought an old brass microscope one of the boys in the carrier platoon had liberated, and my rep for being a bit odd is much strengthened when visitors to our little grass shack find me staring in fascination at the critters in our drinking water. I have discovered that the introduction of a minute portion of vino into their tiny universe sends them into bacchanalian revels—but the least smidgen of grappa knocks them all stone dead...

> The one thing really lacking is women. Some of the lads are making do with a lady of unprepossessing appearance and indeterminate age who hangs around with a herd of goats. Pat opines that the goats are preferable, but then he has peculiar tastes...

On the last night of our stay in the rest area, we officers were permitted to hold a mess dinner attended by six nurses from No. 5 Canadian General Hospital, recently landed in Sicily. It was a very circumspect affair, the highlight of which was a sing-song. But at the witching hour of 8:00 PM the nurses were loaded into jeeps and, escorted by their matron and our colonel, driven back to the virtuous environs of the hospital.

Nevertheless, this tantalizing and fleeting contact with Canadian girls was a tremendous highlight in our dour existence. One of the girls, a brown-haired, snub-nosed lass named Betty, actually spent several minutes talking to me about Saskatoon, where we had both once lived. A major soon snatched her away but by that time I had, naturally enough, fallen in love. I lived in hopes that Betty and I would meet again under less trammelled circumstances. I dreamed of being heroically wounded so I could come under her tender care in hospital, and I composed a number of rather cloying love poems in her honour.

The end of August also marked the end of our period of rest and relaxation. We were in good physical fettle from three weeks of more-or-less virtuous deprivation, and we had learned a new and important military truth: The infantry soldier remains the most important element of any army during battle, when his praises can hardly be sung loudly enough, but when the battle ends he can become an embarrassment, even an encumbrance, to the command structure—something to be put away in a box until the time for bloodshed comes again.

ON SEPTEMBER I we were ordered to move to a concentration area on the Straits of Messina, in preparation for the invasion of mainland Italy. Soon after dawn our convoy drew its trail in dust down to the Catania plains then northward along the coastal highway. As the day aged we could look across the narrowing expanse of the straits and see the purple loom of the massive mountains of Calabria in the distance. That night we lay in bivouacs in a dry watercourse not far from Messina, and on the morrow began the now-familiar ritual of organizing ourselves into serials for an assault landing.

But the mood this time was vastly different from what it had been when we were preparing to go ashore in Sicily. There was none of the high-spirited anticipation we had experienced on the *Derbyshire*. The evening before the crossing Al Park and Paddy Ryan showed up at BHQ ostensibly to share a bottle of scotch Doc had conjured up. We drank and joked and laughed, but the jokes were laboured and the laughter hollow. Eventually Paddy brought up the real reason for the visit.

"What about it, Squib... you must get all sorts of top-flight gen from up above... Will *Tedeschi* be laying for us on the beaches? What d'you think?"

I shrugged with feigned indifference, for I did not want even to imagine what it would be like if the Germans seriously opposed the landing.

"Who can tell? Those assholes at Corps Intelligence don't seem to have a clue... How would *I* know?"

"What odds anyhow?" Al interjected almost angrily. His usually open countenance had a closed and shrouded look. "What frigging odds? When you gotta go... you gotta go and, kid, we gotta go! Let's have another wallop of that scotch."

How had we changed so much so soon? Only six weeks earlier we had plunged headlong into battle with joyful abandon. Now we would continue to fight primarily because we had no choice.

We drained the bottle and were singing the saccharine Big Band songs of 1939 when we were drowned out by Eighth Army's massed artillery as it began firing the preparatory barrage across the narrow strait.

The actual assault, which began at dawn on September 3, proved to be a massive anticlimax. The only show of opposition to the battalion's landing craft as they puttered across came from a flight of Fiat fighters that swept in from the east, danced prettily in the high sky out of range of our anti-aircraft guns, dropped their bombs harmlessly in the sea and headed home content with this gesture of defiance.

We landed without opposition, reorganized, and struck inland up the black face of the towering Aspromonte massif with orders to seize the heights and defend the beachhead against an anticipated counterattack; but there seemed to be no Germans about, and since the Italian troops manning the coastal defences already knew that Mussolini had fallen, they were in no mood to die heroically in a lost cause.

As the regimental column laboured upward like an attenuated khaki-coloured snake, another descended parallel to it, this one bluish-green in hue. The Italian soldiers came down from the hills, not like members of a defeated army but in a mood of fiesta, marching raggedly along with their personal possessions slung about them, filling the air with laughter and song. For them the war was over.

This cascade of happy warriors kept me and my section busier than the proverbial cat on a hot tin roof as we laboured to identify the many different units hell-bent on surrender, while at the same time trying to ascertain what hostile forces, if any, might still be holding out.

By noon next day we had struggled eighteen miles into the heart of the high mountains and, at an altitude of five thousand feet, found ourselves in a world which by contrast with Sicily seemed incredible. Gone were the skeletal olive trees and cactus, replaced by thick, leafy forests of chestnut, oak and beech. Gone too were the heat and drought. During the next few days it rained steadily and massively. It was so wet that fires could hardly be persuaded to burn and we huddled in our thin tropical clothing under dripping trees and shivered through bitter nights.

My section, ever alert for self-serving opportunities, discovered a mountain retreat belonging to the paramilitary Blackshirts, and in it quantities of the famous shirts themselves. These were much thicker and warmer than ours— which explains how it came about that, shortly thereafter, a patrol of the 48th Highlanders sighted a group of armed Blackshirts skulking through the forest. The Highlanders promptly called down artillery fire on this "infiltrating enemy force," thereby starting a flap that swept through the whole brigade and sent everyone scuttling for his weapon. Fortunately, the 48th captured no prisoners, so nobody outside my section ever learned the truth. I hardly felt it was *my* duty to become a tattle-tale, particularly since the black-shirted ones returned with a special gift for me, a portable typewriter which became, and remained, my joy throughout the war years.

While we were immured in the dripping Aspromonte forests, great events were taking place elsewhere. Late on September 8 Marshal Badoglio, Mussolini's successor, announced Italy's unconditional surrender, and next morning we learned that the U.S. Fifth Army had begun landing on the beaches of Salerno, not far south of Naples. These two events seemed to presage a quick end to the war in Italy, and such was the optimism engendered by that prospect that some of us even thought we could detect the early collapse of Germany looming as a consequence.

Fifth Army's landing had been designed to trap the bulk of the eleven German divisions then in Italy in the foot of the peninsula, whither it was believed they would have concentrated to counter the threat of Eighth Army's invasion. The Fifth planned to slice through the ankle from Salerno to the Adriatic Coast, putting this entire German force into "the bag."

However, when the Fifth went ashore the Germans immediately counterattacked in force and it soon became evident that the invaders would do well to hold their beachhead and avoid being driven back into the sea. The Eighth, whose original role had been to act as bait for the Germans—bait the enemy had declined to accept—was now ordered to speed north to the assistance of the beleaguered Fifth. The Eighth was later severely criticized in the USA for taking too long to carry out this rescue mission, but those of us who took part in that gruelling 300-mile thrust up the mountainous spine of Italy were more than content with our accomplishment.

Although the Germans did not at first oppose us in the flesh, they had done as thorough a job of demolition as has been seen in modern warfare. Not a bridge along the few snake-gutted highways, byways and even mountain tracks remained undestroyed. There was hardly a culvert or an overhanging cliff that had not been demolished to form an obstacle. And everywhere—along the road verges, at blown bridges, in the exits from roads and tracks, even in the few level fields where vehicles could be dispersed and men could camp—were mines, mines and more mines.

At the end of the first day of the northward trek I was directing a column of supply trucks off the main road into a stone-walled farmyard. The entrance gap was narrow and one large truck, making too sharp a turn, threatened to pin me to the wall with its front fender. As my mouth opened to scream at the driver, a rear wheel ran over a Teller mine.

A savage force crushed me back against the wall then slammed me forward against the truck with such ferocity that I lost consciousness. When dim awareness began to return, I knew beyond doubt that I was dead. I seemed to hear the distant but mighty roaring of the sea in some vast cave, but could see nothing except a shimmering, translucent haze in which I appeared to float weightlessly. There was no pain, and in fact I felt euphoric—like a disembodied spirit drifting in some other worldly void. Intensely curious about this new state of being into which I had been so summarily dispatched, I allowed myself to drift toward the luminous edge of the haze . . .

. . . and staggered out of a pall of dust and smoke to fall full length over the body of a man whose head had been blown off.

Someone grabbed my arm and pulled me across the road into the ditch beyond. Then Dicky Bird was bending over me, his lips working furiously but soundlessly. He vanished momentarily, to return with a precious bottle of whisky which he began to pour down my throat.

"My goodness *gracious*, Squib, you should have *seen* yourself!" he told me some time later. "You popped out of that dust cloud as white as a rat in a *flour* barrel, and with the *silliest* expression on your face . . . like a girl who's just been *kissed* for the first time."

If kiss it was, then it was very nearly the kiss of death. Seven men were wounded by the explosion and two killed. We survivors had been incredibly lucky. The truck was carrying a ton of 3-inch mortar bombs which, by all the laws of probability, should have exploded too.

Apart from being severely bruised and temporarily deafened, I suffered no real injuries; but within three days we lost eight vehicles and more than twenty casualties to mines of one kind or another.

As we continued north, blown bridges stopped all vehicle movement with the exception of motorcycles and the occasional jeep which could be manhandled over or around the demolitions. The leading infantry units therefore had to proceed on foot, and since time was of the essence, they slogged wearily along for endless hours. I was able to avoid some of this ordeal by virtue of sharing the I-section's Norton motorbike with Sergeant Richmond.

On September 10 the rifle companies staggered into the small coastal town of Catanzaro Marina, having marched sixty miles in two days and nights. The men were at the end of their tether, yet within the hour Kennedy was ordered to strike inland to the city of Catanzaro itself, which lay in a high saddle between 3,000-foot peaks some twenty miles from its port.

Our advance along the coastal road had been unopposed thus far, but in the mountainous interior overlooking our route many units of the Italian army awaited the outcome of the Salerno battle, and the consequences of Badoglio's capitulation, before deciding whether to surrender or to continue with the war. According to an Italian lieutenant who surrendered to us at Catanzaro Marina, Catanzaro itself was heavily garrisoned, but the lieutenant did not know whether or not the forces there were prepared to fight.

I told Kennedy what I had learned, and he muttered angrily as he stared at the map spread before him.

"*No* artillery... *no* tanks... *no* transport... not even any anti-tank guns... and the men are beat. Hell's bells, we can't just go blundering up into those mountains hoping for the best!"

He turned toward me and his light-blue eyes glinted ominously.

"Well, Squib, somebody's got to do a recce, and the only mechanized unit I've got is you and your motorbike. Take someone on the pillion and find out what in hell is going on."

Which is how Bruce Richmond and I, mounted on one ailing motorcycle, briefly became the vanguard for the glorious Eighth Army.

It was a fine fall day with an azure sky and a sun that warmed but did not sear. As we began chugging up the zigzag road into the mountains, Richmond bellowed in my ear that I shouldn't fret about mines because the Norton was too light to set them off. I did not believe him and was fairly gloomy about our prospects, but as we climbed higher and higher and nothing untoward occurred I began to feel elated. The scenery was superb. Below us the Ionian Sea lay quiescent in a sapphire glare. The mountain maze ahead, shrouded in somnolent shadows, seemed to exude a sweet sense of peace. It was something special to be on our own in such a superbly beautiful no-man's land.

We had climbed perhaps ten miles and had achieved a happily relaxed state of mind when the road abruptly swung around a jutting cliff and brought us face to face with a 75-mm anti-tank gun manned by a dozen Italian soldiers.

The Italians, who had of course heard us coming, were nervously fingering their rifles and machine pistols. In the shock of the moment I never even thought about my carbine slung across my back. In fact, I was seized by such an urgent and almost irresistible need to have a pee that nothing much else registered until Richmond muttered sharply in my ear:

"Keep 'er rolling, for Christ's sake! Bluff the bastards!"

Obediently I gunned the engine while he waved a peremptory hand in the direction of still-distant Catanzaro, meanwhile shouting something unintelligible in a commanding tone of voice. Crouching a little, we sped past the muzzle of the gun, whipped gratefully around the next bend—and were appalled to find ourselves confronted by a column of troop-laden trucks completely blocking the road ahead.

"Oh, shit!" snarled Richmond. "Now we're fucked!"

But no... out of the corner of one eye I saw a side road splitting off to the north. I did a skid turn on it and our wild ride continued. Afraid to stop, afraid to turn back, afraid to go on, I prayed we would soon find some sequestered spot where we could hide and catch our breath, quiet our pounding hearts and decide how the devil we were going to extricate ourselves from this cauldron of *minestrone*.

Unfortunately, the road now levelled out and open fields appeared on both sides... fields crowded with tent camps, artillery and transport parks, and large numbers of Italian soldiers who stared at us with a wild surmise as we nipped smartly past. Then we were faced by a barbed-wire roadblock around which there was no detour. The wire, and a sentry with a Beretta submachine gun levelled at us, brought us to a palpitating halt.

At that moment the only thing I had in mind was to avoid being taken prisoner if possible but, if capture was inevitable, to ensure we were taken into custody by someone in authority.

I had an irrational fear of being set upon by a pack of Italian privates lusting to avenge the defeats inflicted on them by Eighth Army.

Bluff had worked once, and in any case there was no other course open to us. In my best or worst *vino Italiano*, I squeakily demanded to be taken to *il generale commandante*.

"*Subito! Subito!*" I added, patting my map case in hopes the sentry would take us for dispatch riders.

I don't know what he took us for—some kind of apparition maybe—but he sent for the sergeant of the guard who in turn sent for an officer who had some English. While we waited I had been madly improvising a story. As haughtily as possible, I informed the officer that we were special emissaries of General Montgomery himself, bearing an urgent dispatch for the commander of the Catanzaro region.

"Ah," he responded, with genuine admiration in his voice. "*Generale* Monta-gomery? *Si*. Ees a very gooda *generale!* I lika him a very more!" with which he cheerfully escorted us to his regimental headquarters, whence we were taken in a staff car to a large *casa* by three amiable officer escorts. There, after a brief pause in an anteroom, we were ushered into the presence of a rotund, much-beribboned general who formally introduced himself as the officer commanding the Mantova Division into whose midst we had blundered.

"Delighted, gentlemen," he said, shaking hands heartily with both of us. "Do please sit down. A glass of wine perhaps, before we talk? Giovanni!"—this to a staff colonel hovering in the background—"some San Severo, if you please."

It was quite a scene: two dusty Canadians sipping excellent wine in the general's quarters, not quite sure if they were awake or dreaming.

In case the general might be a little puzzled that Montgomery's emissaries should be of such lowly rank, I explained that we were merely outriders and would shortly be followed by Brigadier O'Brian-Bennett (the name just sprang to mind), Montgomery's chief-of-staff, who would negotiate the status of the Mantova Division.

"Excellent, gentlemen," said the general affably as he poured more wine for us. "Except for some of the execrable *Fascisti* units, I believe most of the army is ready to abide by the terms of the armistice. I shall be happy to receive your brigadier. Now, is there anything I can do personally for you?"

I was about to say we needed nothing except permission to depart, and a safe conduct, when Sergeant Richmond intervened.

"Excuse me, sir," he said to me with unusual deference. "What about the vehicles General Montgomery wanted?"

Noble Richmond, *clever* Richmond, I thought as I took his meaning.

"Why, yes, General," I said, "there is one small thing you might do..."

UNQUESTIONABLY, ONE OF the highlights of my army career occurred a couple of hours later when, as sole passenger in a chauffeured Alfa Romeo staff car, with Richmond riding escort on the Norton, I led thirty-one huge Italian troop carriers down the mountain to halt them in a neat row at the head of a long column of exhausted Hasty Pees painfully stumbling up the dusty road. Stepping down from the staff car I smartly saluted my astounded commanding officer.

"Beg to report, sir, the general commanding the Mantova Division wishes to have the honour of transporting the

Hastings and Prince Edward Regiment to Catanzaro. And his compliments to you personally, sir, and would you honour him with your presence at dinner this evening at his headquarters? Mess kit would be in order since there will be ladies present."

This was the one and only occasion during the time I knew him that Kennedy seemed to have nothing to say. I was sorely tempted to add: "Cat got your tongue, sir?" But wisdom prevailed.

I still treasure Alex Campbell's comment after the Regiment had completed its journey, riding in style in trucks piloted by the world's most daredevil drivers who, barely three days earlier, had been our avowed enemies.

"By golly, Farley, someday you *might* amount to something, if only as a used-truck dealer."

WE SPENT THE next few days near Catanzaro and as we rested in the cool comfort of pine-clad slopes, surrounded by an entire "enemy" division, there was a marvellous illusion that the war had nearly blown itself out and that what remained was mostly comic opera. Far from encountering animosity or hostility, our problem was to survive the effusive amiability of the Italian soldiers. Everywhere we went they crowded around us as if we were long-lost cousins. The transport drivers who had brought us up the mountain insisted on attaching themselves to us on a permanent basis as honorary Hasty Pees. There were innumerable football games, which the Italians refrained from winning out of excessive courtesy. And there were some excellent parties, during one of which I made friends with a young *capitano* from Milan who pressed his home address on me together with a photograph of his gorgeous younger sister, upon whom he insisted I should call at my earliest convenience.

His English was not perfect but it was enthusiastic.

"She very mucha like the cowboy of your country, and she will be of great desire if you can happily teach her to ride together!"

I'm sure I would have been of great desire too but, alas, I never did get to Milan and so the opportunity went begging.

Major Kennedy reacted to the unreal situation in a way that did not endear him to me. Presumably acting on the assumption that what Richmond and I could do he could do better, he took to setting out at the wheel of his jeep on extended incursions into the as-yet-unliberated territory to the north.

His sole concession to potential dangers was to make me perch precariously on the jeep's bonnet, my feet dangling between the front wheels, to warn him of mines in the road ahead. Since he seldom drove at less than fifty miles an hour, and my eyesight and reflexes were not those of Superman, this had to be the most supremely useless function I had ever been asked to perform. For a long time afterwards I had nightmares of speeding down interminable mountain roads with Kennedy at the wheel while Italian civilians by the roadside screamed mournfully after us, *"Minata! Minata! Pericolo... minata!"*

ALL TOO SOON we were on the move again, but the Germans remained elusive and our principal opponent, apart from mines and demolitions, became disease— malaria and dysentery having been joined by infectious hepatitis to form a triumvirate which caused us considerable casualties. We were now very much "out in the blue," in only tenuous contact with our supply columns and apparently permanently out of touch with Canada, as one of my letters unhappily complains.

No mail for over a month now. One of the horrors of war is the way our mail gets mislaid or waylaid... The problem works both ways too. They only give us one airgraph blank a week, though back in the base area they have so many they use them for bumwad, so don't expect to hear much from yours truly... In your last letter, written two months ago, you say you've been sending 300 cigs a month. Well, I've received one carton in the last *eight* months! They tell us the rest were sunk. Bullshit! They are stolen wholesale by the bastards down the line...

I think the end of the war just *may* be in sight. In men and material we have the Jerries by the hind tit, and with the Russkies knocking at the western gates Hitler may surrender to our side. Anyway, the betting is we'll all be home early in 1944...

One of the lads in my section, Ivan Gunter, got the Military Medal last week for a job he did in Sicily. They're a great crowd! So far we've had four casualties in the section but all four came back eventually sporting their scars and telling ghastly tales of what it's like in North African convalescent camps. Me, I don't have a scar to show, though I'm now one of the senior surviving lieutenants in the unit. Al Park claims I'm just too insignificant for Jerry to bother with...

The Salerno bridgehead having at last been relieved, we emerged from the mountains into the broad Foggia plains. Lord Tweedsmuir rejoined us here and Ack Ack Kennedy reverted to second-in-command. A small draft of reinforcements also reached us, including a young chap named Luke Reid with whom I had gone to school in Richmond Hill. Although Luke was a year older than me, I found myself treating him in rather avuncular fashion and I arranged to have him posted to the I-section so I could keep an eye on him. I was beginning to think of myself as an "old sweat," and Kennedy may have thought so too because shortly before Tweedsmuir returned to us he had suggested that I begin training a successor. Kennedy might merely have concluded I was due to run out of luck, but I think he was considering promoting me to a captaincy and another job.

When I mentioned this possibility to Doc, he was not overjoyed.

"Jeez, boss! Don't you take no third pip! They'll stick us back out in a rifle company and get the both of us kilt stone dead!"

As it happened, Tweedsmuir decided he wanted no staff changes for awhile; and so to Doc's relief, and—let me be honest—mine as well, we remained at Battalion Headquarters.

OCTOBER 1, a brilliant autumnal day, found us motoring across the Foggia plains toward the already snow-capped peaks of the central Apennines. We were in a carefree mood, for such was the flood of optimism washing down from on high that we fully expected to be driving into Rome within the month.

The high command apparently believed the Germans would offer only light resistance as they withdrew to a defence line in the formidable transverse range of mountains which cuts across the top of the Italian peninsula some two hundred miles north of Rome. Consequently, when the Royal Canadian Regiment, acting as advance guard for our divisional convoy, unexpectedly came under fierce fire from the village of Motta in the foothills bounding the Foggia plains to the north, nobody read the omens aright. Motta was duly taken, but only after a day and night of bloody battle. Furthermore, the Germans stubbornly retained ownership of the heights beyond the town.

When we were ordered to drive them off with one of our famous flank attacks, we found ourselves ignominiously pinned down on an exposed slope by a massive weight of machine-gun and mortar fire. During the night the Germans did withdraw—but of their own volition—and it was in a somewhat subdued state of mind that we occupied their abandoned positions.

The enemy had left a few corpses behind and as usual I had to search them before burial. They turned out to be men of the 1st Paratroop Division, by reputation the most formidable formation in the German army. As if this was not enough to give us pause, one of the dead men carried an uncompleted letter to a friend on the Russian front with this sobering paragraph:

I think there will be no home leave for a long time. I don't expect to see Hanna and the children this year. The Fuhrer has ordered us to hold Rome at all costs. This shouldn't be too hard if you have any idea of the kind of country here. It is made for defence and the Tommies will have to chew their way through us inch by inch, and we will surely make hard chewing...

I considered this letter important enough to send it straight off to the brigade intelligence officer who immediately forwarded it on up the ladder. But optimism still held sway in high places, as the brigade IO ruefully informed me later.

"I got one hell of a rocket back all the way from Corps, accusing me of trying to spread alarm and despondency. I was told not to get my ass in an uproar—that the letter was nothing but soldier's brag!"

With our departure from the plains the weather changed drastically. Suddenly it was the rainy season. We spent the morning after our brush with the paratroopers in another dripping forest under a cold and driving rain against which neither our light clothing nor our supposedly waterproof capes gave any real protection. As we shivered around little tea fires, gloomily considering the future, orders arrived for a flank march parallel to the main road leading into the interior which, after mature consideration, the high-priced help had now concluded the Germans might try to deny to us.

It was growing dark before Tweedsmuir could hold his O-group. Having briefed the company commanders he turned to me in his usual rather deprecatory manner.

"I say, Squib, it may be a bit difficult finding our way in this filthy weather, in darkness, over some fairly rough terrain. Rather a lot to ask of your scouts, eh? Since you're the chief map-wallah, perhaps you'd best take the lead yourself."

I should have told him then that I was not, never had been, nor ever would be one of the world's great navigators, but instead I nodded obediently.

Equipped with a prismatic compass, a soggy Italian map which was next to useless even when dry, a tiny flashlight, and accompanied by the newly arrived Luke Reid to act as my runner, I set forth at the head of a column of about five hundred heavily laden soldiers.

It was a devilishly wet and slippery night. Men stumbled over outcrops of rock and fell into gullies. Morosely they cursed the fates, their loads and doubtless me as well. It was impossible to find a trail. Every compass course I set seemed to lead either to a sheer cliff or a bottomless abyss. Some time after midnight I got the head of the column stuck in a thicket of thorn bushes, and an irate Ack Ack Kennedy shoved his way forward.

"Mowat! Goddamn it, are you lost?"

Benumbed with cold, and miserable with self-pity, I admitted that I was.

"Jesus God! Well, can you get us to the road? To *any* road?"

I mumbled that perhaps I could—if there wasn't a mountain in the way.

"Then do it!"

With Reid faithfully following on my heels, I headed south and an hour later we reached a road which appeared to be the main highway. Kennedy had stayed with me and, since Tweedsmuir was too far back in the column to be easily contacted, he made his own decision.

"Right. The only way we'll ever get out of this goddamn mess is stick to the hard, and bloody well see what happens!"

Picking our way as cautiously and quietly as possible over broken asphalt, the three of us had gone about a quarter of a mile in inky darkness when I froze to the sharp rattle of a weapon being cocked, and almost instantaneously the night exploded.

Half a dozen machine guns ripping out streams of red and yellow tracer had opened fire from our right flank. The nearest was so close that by the flickering light of its muzzle flashes I could see I was under the edge of a roadside cut, from the top of which at least two guns were firing. I saw nothing of Reid as I dived for the ditch but Kennedy landed almost on top of me. We scrunched into the muck as the Brens of the company behind us began coming into action, haphazardly spraying the road and posing almost as great a danger to us as they did to the enemy. But none of the Brens sounded close, and the sickening realization dawned on me that we three had somehow managed to get far ahead of the rest of the column.

The Germans now began to unlimber their mortars, and that brought a quick reply from ours. The din was becoming horrendous, though not loud enough to completely drown out raucous shouts of command from a German on top of the cut bank who could have been no more than a dozen feet from me.

Kennedy's lips were against my ear.

"Don't move a muscle... not a sound... or they'll drop a grenade right onto us..."

It was a needless warning. Never in my life had I been so anxious to remain unnoticed. "There is nothing in this world," I wrote later, "so humiliating, demeaning, frustrating and bloody terrifying as to lie with your nose in the mud while both the Huns and your own side fight a battle over your cringing flesh."

Luckily for us, it was largely a blind battle. Darkness, rain and fog made aimed fire almost impossible, and even the illuminating flares which the enemy was sending up were nearly useless. However, the sheer volume of steel the Germans were pouring down the road made the battalion's situation untenable. The response from our own troops began to fade and grow more distant and, with a sinking heart, I realized they were pulling out.

Kennedy realized it too.

"Better make a break ... stay much longer we'll be caught ... try it across the road."

I thought of Reid somewhere behind me but dared not shout to him and so could only hope he would reach the same conclusion as Kennedy and I.

Kennedy touched my arm and then was gone. I rolled to my knees and plunged into the blackness. Seconds later my flailing feet shot out from under me as I tumbled into the steep bed of a raging streamlet. I could hear splashing ahead of me and, crouching on hands and knees, made my way toward the sound. Kennedy had again injured the leg which had been wounded at Nissoria, but together we worked our way downstream until we reckoned ourselves out of the danger zone.

It was dawn before we found the Regiment again. It had taken up defence positions on some hills to the north of the road a mile from where we had been ambushed. Nobody had seen anything of Reid. Much later I was to learn that he had flopped into the ditch some yards behind me, at a point where there was no protecting cut bank. Unwilling to take the risk of making a break for it when we did, he had lain doggo until first light when the Germans spotted and captured him. But at the time I was sure he had been killed in this, his first hour of battle, and for weeks afterwards I was haunted by the guilty conviction that real responsibility for his death was mine— that I had fatally failed him as a man and as a friend. The relief I felt when word finally came through that he was a prisoner, and alive, was indescribable.

Tweedsmuir was making plans for a daylight attack on the German positions when a tired and muddy brigade liaison officer arrived on foot—no vehicles could reach our position—bearing new orders. We were now told to undertake an even longer and more ambitious flank march through yet bigger mountains to capture the town of Celenza, nineteen miles away as the crow might fly.

Whoever conceived that operation must have been totally out of touch with reality. We had been skirmishing with the Germans in rain and fog for two days and nights, wet and cold most of the time, existing on the skimpy rations each of us carried in his pack, getting low on ammo, without sleep, and without radio communications with our own forces. If Kennedy had been in command I think he might have refused the order; but this was just the sort of mission that appealed to Tweedsmuir's unregenerate romanticism. It was the kind of do-or-die challenge he could not resist.

Fatalistic with fatigue, we plodded off into a new maze of rocky peaks and sodden valleys. And I was again the appointed navigator. Possibly Tweedsmuir was giving me a chance to redeem myself. Possibly he simply had not paused to weigh the consequences.

Through the next forty-eight hours we wandered in the wilderness. Most of the time I knew roughly where we were, but it proved virtually impossible to go where we wanted to go. We were forever being circumvented by stretches of impassable terrain. We found no enemy to fight—only mountains to climb and new downpours to shudder under. Food was a dream, and so was sleep. All links to the rear were broken and Brigadier Graham was again left to bite his nails and wonder if he had lost us forever.

There were a few brighter moments. One came when we stumbled on a stone hut in this otherwise empty world and the old goatherd who lived there in splendid isolation freely gave dippers of milk and the last bits of his scanty supply of bread to the famished soldiers who straggled past. Then there was an encounter with an Italian doctor in flight from the Germans and unaccountably leading a troop of mules. Not only did he treat our injured, he also volunteered his scraggly beasts to carry our heavy weapons.

At dawn on October 6, when we were finally within striking distance of Celenza and separated from it only by Mount Miano, a high ridge ten miles long, Tweedsmuir sent out a fighting patrol which brought back the unwelcome news that the ridge appeared to be heavily defended. Nothing daunted, Tweedsmuir doggedly determined to outflank Mount Miano.

We tried—but we had not gone far when an impenetrable fog descended on us and, not to mince matters, I got lost again and led the bone-weary troops a considerable distance in the wrong direction. As night fell, I discovered my error but was afraid to tell anyone except the commanding officer, for fear of being drawn and quartered on the spot. Tweedsmuir was remarkably forbearing. He looked at me sadly and remarked: "I say, Squib, rather a poor show, don't you know."

It was a mild rebuke but in my dishevelled and exhausted state of mind it rankled more than a thorough bawling-out. All through that wet and dreadful night I brooded until by dawn I was in the grip of an irrational compulsion to redeem myself.

Tweedsmuir was dozing and shivering in the meagre shelter of an abandoned goat pen when I approached him with the proposal that I lead a mule-mounted patrol consisting of myself, three of my scouts and the doctor to act as muleteer, and reconnoitre a route straight across the crest of Mount Miano. He concurred in this hare-brained scheme with such alacrity that I concluded he would have agreed to almost anything if only it meant ridding himself of my presence.

My resolution hardened. This time, by God, it was *going* to be do or die! Which is how it came to pass that the 1st Squadron of Mowat's Mounted Mules ambled off into the grey drizzle—not cautiously skulking under cover, but heading brazenly out into the open across a flat plateau directly toward the lowering bulk of Mount Miano.

One of our little party was determined to accomplish a memorable deed, or perish in the attempt, but it was *not* George Langstaff, my premier scout. Goading his mule into a trot, he hauled up alongside me, his craggy face creased with anxious lines.

"What the hell! You want every Jerry on that mountain to see us coming?"

I fixed him with my steeliest eye.

"Yes, *Private* Langstaff, that's exactly what I want. And they'll think we're nothing but a bunch of Eyetie farmers and pay no attention. See?"

He looked at me with what I took to be awe-struck admiration, until he said: "Holy shit, Junior! You've blown your stack!"

With which, and a fatalistic shrug, he fell back into line and we plodded damply on.

Don Quixote would have been proud of us. *I* was proud of us when at last we reached the foot of the wooded slopes of the ridge without having drawn a single shot. Shrouded by mist and drizzle, we had successfully managed to masquerade as a party of civilians. Tensely we made our way upward through the dripping trees until at last we heard vehicles grumbling on a road which, the map had indicated, ran along the crest.

Leaving the doctor to keep the mules quiet, the rest of us inched slowly forward until we could see the road. For the moment it appeared to be deserted. Hurriedly we dragged a fallen tree trunk across it and I placed my two other scouts, Lyall Emigh and Keith Close, with two Brens to cover the approaches from both directions. Leaving Langstaff in charge, I raced down to the doctor and told him to take one of the mules and get back to the Regiment as fast as possible. I gave him a hastily scribbled note bearing this brave message:

"Have cut main Celenza road on Mount Miano. Will keep it cut until relieved."

The departing clatter of the mule's hooves was still in my ears when I heard the stutter of an approaching motorcycle on the road above. I pounded back up the slope expecting at every instant to hear the Brens open fire. Instead there came the squeal of tires braking hard, a challenge, a moment's pregnant silence, and then a startled shout.

"Langstaff! You crazy old bugger! Where in hell've you bastards been? And why in hell are you pointing them goddamn gats at me?"

I would willingly drop the curtain at this point, but Truth is a hard mistress and will not be denied.

When I stumbled onto the road, it was to find my scouts sheepishly trying to explain themselves to one of our Headquarters Company dispatch riders. Bewildered, I joined them and in due course heard the details of what was for me a sorry tale.

Headquarters Company—the battalion supply and maintenance group—had been left behind with all its vehicles near Motta four days earlier. As time went on and there was no word of our whereabouts, the company set out to discover for itself what had happened to us. Meeting with no difficulties except some unguarded demolitions which were detoured, the column motored unconcernedly along until it reached Mount Miano.

The "enemy" reported by Tweedsmuir's fighting patrol had in fact consisted of our own cooks, clerks, drivers and storemen, preparing bivouacs against the day when the battalion would see fit to emerge from its travail in wilderness.

I believe I had reason to feel the fates had done me in the eye. Yet later in the day when I tried to elicit some sympathy from Paddy Ryan, he was unresponsive.

"You were goddamn lucky, Squib. If you'd stayed with us *we'd* have killed you. And if there'd been Jerries on Miano *they'd* have killed you. You should count your blessings..."

PERHAPS GOADED BY the jibes of the Headquarters Company men, Lyall Emigh and Keith Close determined to redeem the I-section's honour. A day after our ill-starred arrival on Mount Miano, they saw an opportunity to do so.

The Germans were then believed to be holding the line of the Fortore River about five miles west of Celenza. Anticipating that we might have to make an attack across this river, I sent Close and Emigh off to look for crossing places.

The river level was low and no Germans appeared to be around, so the two young men waded to the other side, then cautiously climbed to the hill town of Macchia, which turned out to be free of Germans too. Here they were greeted as liberators by the populace, and fêted and vinoed to such an extent that they decided to have a little more of the same by advancing to the next town and liberating it as well.

"It wasn't only fun and games we was after," Close later explained to me. "*Somebody* had to put the I-section back on the map, and, begging your pardon, sir, it looked like it was up to us. We figured if we could find a hole in the Jerry line, the Div could bust right through and we'd all come out covered with roses..."

However, as they approached a final hill before the village of St. Elia, they beheld a khaki-clad figure waving at them from the far edge of a field of grain. It seemed they had been forestalled. They walked toward the stranger to pass the time of day and learn if there were any more unliberated towns around. It was not until they were only a hundred yards apart that Close began to have doubts.

"Lyall," he said sharply, "does that guy's uniform look queer to you?"

"Jesus, yes! Maybe we should start shooting!"

They dropped to their bellies but had no time to aim or fire before "what sounded like a million Spandaus opened up on us, trimming the grain right over our heads as good as any mowing machine!"

"What in hell do we do now?" Close muttered plaintively as he embraced the hard earth.

"Hold up your map case... high! And wave the jeezly thing like it had wings!"

The Germans ceased fire and the would-be liberators got warily to their feet to find they had become prisoners of war.

They did not go into captivity with dignity. They were dispatched to the rear, pushing and pulling at the outpost's ration mule while the German guards convulsed themselves with merriment. The scouts' patience had worn thin by the time they were bundled into a motorcycle sidecar. The burly driver was armed with a rifle slung across his shoulders and a pistol at his belt, while the guard, riding pillion, carried a machine carbine cradled in his lap. Occasionally he shoved the muzzle into Close's ribs and grinned.

Seething with a mixture of rage at the Germans and disgust with themselves, the scouts could endure no more. As one, they suddenly jumped their captors and all four men fell in a tangle on the road.

As the driver struggled to free his pistol, Close grabbed the muzzle of the slung rifle and pulled it down with such force that the butt flew between the driver's legs with pile-driver force, leaving him with no further interest in the battle. Seizing the pistol, Close then clubbed the guard who was about to empty his carbine into Emigh.

An armoured half-track now rumbled into view, and the scouts fled over the crest of a nearby hill, pursued by angry shouts and a fusillade of shots. Below them lay a valley with a small stream running down its centre. There was no time to scale the far slopes so the fugitives leapt into the stream, crouched low, and were scuttling along it when Close spotted a dark shadow under the bank. He yanked Emigh by the arm and the two men dived into the shelter of a cave.

It was no natural cave. The scouts were appalled to find themselves sharing a tiny, man-made cavern with several crates of startled chickens who looked as if they were about to protest the intrusion with a wild alarum. Neither man dared move a muscle.

Three times they saw German jackboots stomp past the entrance, and each time their eyes swivelled, horror-stricken, toward the restless but, mercifully, still-silent birds.

Dusk came. Again the scouts heard footsteps, then a hairy face thrust itself into view. It belonged to an aged farmer who had contrived this sanctuary in which to keep his precious flock of hens safe from the *Tedeschi*. This evening when he came to feed them, he found himself the prisoner of two wild-eyed Canadians.

At first Emigh and Close did not know what to do with him. They did not trust him to serve as their guide back to the Fortore, and for the same reason dared not let him go free. Finally Emigh came up with a solution. He ordered the old man to make his own way to our lines and to bring back a well-armed Canadian patrol. If he failed to do so or betrayed the two men to the Germans, he was warned, his precious flock would be massacred to the last hen. In the face of this horrendous threat, the old fellow went forlornly off into the night to do his best.

Astonishingly he managed to cross the lines and find a Canadian unit to whom he told his story; but the soldiers did not believe it. Disconsolate and fearing the worst, the old man returned to the cave to report his failure. It was already past midnight and Close and Emigh were desperate enough by then to risk using him as a guide. In what must have seemed to him like a nightmare that would never end, the old man once again made his way through the German outposts to the Canadian unit which had rejected him before.

When Close and Emigh returned next morning, they brought him along. Before he was turned loose to go home to his *casa* and his chickens, we so loaded him with bully beef, cigarettes and chocolate that he could hardly stagger.

As for Close and Emigh—for some time afterwards all one had to do to send either of them into a state of shock was to sneak up in an unguarded moment and cackle like a startled hen.

THE PROPHECY CONTAINED in the dead paratrooper's letter became a harsh reality as winter drew on. Our approach to Campobasso, capital of the central Apennine region (and the city from which we were supposed to debouch northwestward down the mountain slopes to Rome) slowed to a crawl in the face of increasingly tough enemy opposition, rugged terrain and steadily worsening weather. Veritably, we were reduced to "chewing our way... inch by inch."

By the middle of October, 1st Brigade had only just reached the vicinity of a hill town called Ferrazzano which clung, Assoro-like, to the top of a crag some ten miles from Campobasso.

This time the mountain-goat role went to the 48th Highlanders. They scaled the crag and drove off the Germans, but did not pause to clear the town itself, leaving this task to us. Tweedsmuir dispatched a platoon to occupy the place.

With Doc to keep me company I decided to go along, not because I craved excitement but because I hoped to spend a few hours enjoying the shelter of a roof and, with luck, the warmth of a fire and a good hot feed.

The platoon was led by a recently arrived reinforcement, Lieutenant Gerry Swayle, an earnest and slightly myopic young man sporting a pair of steel-rimmed spectacles, who shared my interests in birds and poetry. As was the way of things in those times, we had already become close friends although we had known one another a bare ten days.

Ferrazzano appeared to have been abandoned by the enemy. As we made our way down its echoing and empty streets, I selected a likely looking house as a temporary headquarters and told Doc to investigate it and also see what he could scrounge in the way of grub. Meantime I went along with Gerry Swayle to examine a crumbling *castello* on the town's walled northern outskirts which looked as if it might be suitable for use as an observation post.

Gerry had already dispersed his platoon by sections to search the rest of the town, so the two of us were alone as we approached the castle. Playing the part of the veteran, I slouched along with assumed sang-froid; but Gerry, being a new boy, insisted on an intent advance from doorway to doorway, with his Tommy gun at the ready, exactly as he had been taught in battle school.

We were ten or fifteen yards from the castle's open gates when an engine unexpectedly roared, there was a clash of gears, and an open car shot out of the inner courtyard heading directly for us. I recognized it as being German and turned to run, but its occupants' reflexes were faster than mine. The passenger in the front seat raised a Schmeisser submachine gun and let fly a staccato burst.

I felt a thudding blow on my back, and the impact spun me about and flung me sprawling into the filthy, open gutter where I lay waiting for the next burst to finish me off.

There was no second burst. Instead Gerry's Tommy hammered thunderously. The car veered, screeched into a skid and smashed sideways against a house front, where it teetered for a moment before rolling slowly over on its side to spill its two occupants onto the rain-washed cobbles, where they lay motionless.

An instant later Gerry was at my side, his hand on my shoulder and his owlish eyes staring anxiously into mine.

"How bad is it, Squib?"

"Don't know," I replied faintly. "Can't feel a thing."

Gingerly he rolled me on my side and eased my small pack off my back. I still felt no pain, so with his gentle assistance I sat up. Still nothing. Slowly and incredulously it dawned on me that I was uninjured.

Innumerable tales have been told in every nominally Christian army about men whose lives were saved because the Bibles they carried in their breast pockets stopped what otherwise would have been fatal bullets. On this occasion *my* life was saved, initially at least, because I had stuffed my small pack with cans of bully beef which I had intended to trade for tastier rations with the inhabitants of Ferrazzano; instead of which they had absorbed or deflected the Schmeisser bullets. For the rest, of course, I owed my continuing existence to Gerry Swayle.

The whole incident had happened much too fast for me to feel fear; and the exhilaration of still being alive was such that the touch of the angel's wing seemed almost trivial, almost a thing to laugh about. Not many days later I was to think of it quite differently.

Drawn by the firing, some of Swayle's men came to our rescue at the run. They searched the castle but found it empty. The erstwhile occupants of the car had evidently been the last of the German garrison. We never knew why they had lingered, but when I examined the bodies I found that the passenger was a staff captain from the Hermann

Göring Division, carrying a marked map showing many of the German dispositions in front of Campobasso. He also had two bottles of cognac in a wicker case, one of which was still intact.

While Swayle's runner hastened back to the battalion with the marked map for dispatch to Divisional Intelligence, Gerry and I returned to the house where I had left Doc Macdonald.

Doc had performed his usual magic. We found him in a warm kitchen assisting three cheerful and voluble women to pluck a brace of fowl while various pots came to the boil on a big, charcoal-fired stove. It appeared that my shattered cans of bully beef, which I had abandoned to the town's stray dogs, would not be needed after all.

But *I* was needed—somewhere else. While Swayle, Doc and I were taking our ease and filling our bellies, in Ferrazzano the battalion had received orders to pass through the 48th and assist the Royal Canadian Regiment in the attack on Campobasso. Tweedsmuir's brigade radio link was out of order and, since he could not contact the commanding officer of the RCR by any other means, he decided to send an officer to "liaise" between the two units. This officer should have been me but I was nowhere to be found, so Major Ack Ack Kennedy went in my stead.

As Kennedy was making his way along a road leading toward the supposed positions of the RCR, he came under heavy mortar fire. It seemed wise to make a detour, so he sprinted across an open field to the shelter of a sunken hedgerow and proceeded forward under its protection. At the same time a German infantry squad was approaching in the opposite direction. Kennedy walked right into it and promptly became a prisoner of war.

Some weeks later, having escaped from a Germany-bound prison train, and working his way southward for many days through the central mountains, he crossed back into our lines and rejoined the battalion. When he met me again, he was a little touchy about my unauthorized absence from the scene in front of Campobasso.

ON OCTOBER 14 the Germans abandoned Campobasso, and the Royal Canadian Regiment occupied the almost-undamaged city overlooking the deep valley of the Biferno River, to whose precipitous northern slopes the enemy had withdrawn into well-prepared positions which were part of a new and unexpected defence line that gartered the Italian "leg" at its narrowest part, a hundred miles to the *south* of Rome, and before which the advance of the Fifth and Eighth armies was grinding to a halt.

We now went into reserve and were sent to bivouac in a bleak and windy field, while the administrative and headquarters staffs of Corps and Division moved into snug winter quarters in the many fine modern buildings with which Mussolini had graced Campobasso. However, the city was still within range of some German guns and occasional nuisance shellings disturbed the staff officers and base troops, so 1st Brigade was ordered to use its rest period to "sterilize" a number of small villages on our side of the Biferno which were suspected of harbouring German artillery observation posts.

We had barely pitched our makeshift tents when Tweedsmuir was told to clean out three villages on our sector. He sent Able Company off to take Montagano, which clung to a promontory in a northward-looping bend of the river; and the carrier platoon to occupy San Stefano, a hamlet in the valley far below us. Then, as an afterthought, it seemed, he told me to make a jeep patrol to Ripalimosani, a mile outside of San Stefano.

Able drove a German standing patrol out of Montagano, and then had to hold the place through eight days of heavy shellfire which cost the company many casualties.

The carrier platoon encountered mines and mortar fire on the approaches to San Stefano, forcing the crews to reverse their light armoured vehicles and withdraw.

As for me, accompanied only by Doc Macdonald, and unaware of what was taking place elsewhere, I drove nonchalantly into Ripalimosani where, to the wild pealing of church bells, Doc and I were received as liberators by an ecstatic mob. The mayor, a returned émigré from Chicago, escorted us into the town hall for an alcoholic and heroic welcome. I enjoyed the experience so much that I paid little heed when the mayor casually mentioned that a German platoon, which had been occupying the town, had withdrawn less than an hour earlier. Not until next day did I appreciate how well my luck was holding.

Early the following morning Gerry Swayle and his platoon were told to occupy San Stefano. It was assumed the enemy rearguards had all withdrawn across the Biferno overnight and Gerry would meet with no resistance. I saw him just before he started off and told him about the joys of liberating Ripalimosani.

"Ask for the Spumanti," I advised him. "It's terrific stuff and they seem to have enough around to float a battleship."

He gave me his owlish look, grinning cheerfully as he took his place at the head of his platoon. Then he led his men down the white, gravelled road that curved and twisted toward the little village... directly into an ambush of half a dozen enfilading machine guns supported by heavy mortars.

The two rearward sections of the platoon managed to gain the shelter of the roadside ditches where they were pinned until darkness enabled them to belly-crawl away. But Gerry, and every man of his leading section, was hit. The lucky ones were killed outright. The rest died slowly of their wounds, for it was impossible to reach them.

Their bodies lay strewn on the road for five days before a full-scale battalion attack finally took San Stefano and allowed us to recover our dead.

I assisted the padre and the burial party. Despite the chill, wet weather, the bodies had bloated to the point where they had stretched their stained, stinking and saturated clothing sausage-tight. They did not look like men anymore. They had become obscene parodies of men. Somebody handed me Gerry's broken spectacles, and for the first time since the real war began for me my eyes filled with tears. For the first time I truly understood that the dead... were dead.

A day or two later I wrote in a letter home:

It's hard for guys my age to grasp that nobody lives forever. Dying is just a word until you find out differently. That's trite, but horribly true. The first few times you almost get nicked you take it for granted you are naturally immortal. The next few times you begin to wonder. After that you start looking over your shoulder to make sure old Lady Luck is still around. Then, if you're still in one piece, you wonder when she is going to scram to parts unknown... A young guy named Swayle came up to us three weeks ago, fresh out from Blighty, and before he really knew what in hell it was all about, he ended up a pile of perforated meat along with seven of his men. Why him? Why them? And when will it be you? That's the sort of question you ask yourself.

As if clearing the villages had not been enough to demand of us, the remainder of our rest period was given over to "aggressive" patrolling deep into the German defences across the Biferno. The purpose of this, so said the staff, was to keep the enemy off balance. Whether it did or not, it certainly made him angry. Patrolling became a tit-for-tat sort of thing. Every time we penetrated his lines he would retaliate with a patrol into ours. Our men were better at this kind of hit-and-run warfare than the more regimented German soldiers, but we were to discover that even our best were outclassed by the Italian partisans.

I knew very little about the partisans, apart from occasional references to them in Intelligence reports, until one morning George Langstaff returned from a single-handed patrol behind the German lines, accompanied by a tall, saturnine, eagle-nosed Italian of about thirty who introduced himself as Giovanni, which was his code name and the only one he answered to.

Giovanni was a communist who had first been an anti-Fascist, then an anti-German guerrilla, leading a partisan band among the crags of the high Apennines. He had been captured by the Fascists and tortured, as livid scars bore witness.

A few days before we arrived at Campobasso, he and his group had been attempting to blow up one of the Biferno bridges when they were surprised by a German armoured column. During the ensuing fight most of the partisans were killed. Several wounded men who attempted to surrender were shot on the spot by their German captors. One might reasonably have concluded that, as one of the few survivors, Giovanni would have been content to take things easy for awhile. I thought so anyway, but then I did not know my man.

A modest fellow, but radiating confidence, he politely shrugged off questions about his exploits and it was some time before I discovered even these few facts about him. He had small interest in the past. He only wanted to get on with the war against the *Tedeschi,* and to this end he suggested that I let him work for us. Such an arrangement between front-line troops and Italian civilians was strictly forbidden on the grounds that they might prove to be double agents, but I decided that even if Giovanni *was* working both sides, he could do us no real harm, and he might be able to do us considerable good. Besides, I liked the man.

He proved to be of inestimable value. As head of an unofficial intelligence service, he and one or two companions, who appeared, as it were, out of the mists, made more than thirty excursions on our behalf behind the German lines. The information they brought back was exact, detailed and abundant enough to give 1st Brigade Intelligence (my friend the brigade intelligence officer was the only other officer privy to our secret) a reputation for almost superhuman sapience.

Giovanni never came back empty-handed. In addition to information, he often had an escaped prisoner of war in tow—a U.S. airman, a British survivor of Tobruk, once even a merchant captain from Cardiff, captured after his ship was sunk on the Malta run. If he could not find one of our people to rescue, he would bring a captured German instead. Of these I particularly remember an artillery ober-lieutenant who was so glad to get out of Giovanni's hands and into ours that he broke down and sobbed. Giovanni was not gentle with the enemy.

He asked nothing from us and would accept nothing except food, most of which I suspect he gave away to needy peasants behind the German lines.

At the end of October our "rest period" ended and we were ordered to cross the Biferno and strike deep into the German defence zone. On a rain-dark night we slipped and slithered down to a roaring river swollen by the endless downpours and spanned by a decrepit power dam over which the waters foamed so fiercely that the Germans must have assumed the dam was impassable and so had failed to defend or even mine it. Giovanni knew better. We followed him across in single file, perilously balancing in sucking, knee-deep water. Then we struck across country into forested and sombre heights toward a mountain town called Molise, some twelve miles north of the Biferno.

Again it was my job to lead the way, but this time my navigation did not fail, for although nobody except my I-section men was aware of it, Giovanni was the actual pilot. I concealed this, not so I could reap the kudos for a job well done, but because some of my fellow officers might have balked at following an avowed communist, and an Italian one at that, deep into enemy territory.

At dawn we surprised the garrison of Molise and took the place without suffering a single casualty. However, the discomfited Germans retaliated by subjecting our positions to a furious bombardment. Their gunfire was uncannily accurate and we lost six killed and fourteen wounded in the first few hours... before Giovanni, testing the undercurrents, discovered that we were in a Fascist hotbed. As a result of the brisk elimination by Giovanni of the mayor and several of his cohorts who had been informing the Germans of our dispositions through a concealed field telephone line, the fire became much less accurate, though it remained intense.

One morning Giovanni and I were together at the window of a house overlooking the town square when a signaller started across it with a message in his hand. There was a tremendous *swoosh* and a stunning crash as a 15-cm shell landed in the middle of the square. As the dust and smoke swirled clear, the signaller emerged in view, standing as if rooted to the spot. Then slowly, slowly, he began to bend backward from the waist. With a soundless gush his guts spilled from him to drape his legs as if in bloody vermicelli. A shell fragment had virtually cut him in half, leaving only his spine and a handful of skin and muscle linking the two portions of his body.

Giovanni cursed softly. Next morning he appeared out of nowhere, as was his custom, and handed me a carefully drawn map upon which he had exactly located every gun position of a battery of 15-cm German howitzers. I passed the map references to our artillery observer who promptly organized a divisional "stonk"—the simultaneous fire of one medium and three field regiments.

The following day Giovanni smilingly reported that two of the guns had been destroyed and the rest hurriedly removed to a more distant site, leaving behind six Gothic wooden crosses, each topped with a helmet, over six new graves.

"Your guns, they blew them up," he told me with a satisfied glint in his eye. "But me, *I* killed those pigs!"

Shortly thereafter we were relieved and sent to a village called Castropignano in what had now become the rear area. I assumed Giovanni would accompany us but he politely declined. For us the war might temporarily be over, but for him it went on as before. Having acquired the nucleus of a new guerrilla band and having equipped himself and his companions with captured German weapons, he intended to go back into action on his own.

Our parting was emotional. He presented each member of the I-section with a gift—mine was a filigree bracelet "for your girl in Canada"—after which he embraced us and we drank grappa to the toast he proposed.

"*Arrividerci,* comrades! Good luck! Good loving! Good drinking!... and good hunting!"

FOR THE FIRST time since leaving England we folded up our groundsheets and took refuge in billets. Although hardly palatial, the bomb-blasted and shell-shattered houses of Castropignano (familiarly known to us as Castropigface) on the north bank of the Biferno at least offered some protection from the biting rain and snow squalls sweeping down from the white-sheathed mountains.

Winter had come upon us with a vengeance. The rivers rose and washed away the pontoon bridges with which our engineers had spanned the Biferno, cutting us off from the rear areas. Winter clothing was slow in arriving and so we made do with whatever we could find. Doc supplied himself and me with short coats made out of army blankets by the local tailor, who charged four cans of bully beef or five pounds of flour for his labour.

Despite the best efforts of the military authorities to stop it, we and the Italian civilians were soon living largely by mutual barter. Doc, who had become the unofficial I-section victualler, made daily expeditions far afield to exchange *scarpe* (boots), sugar, flour, bully, cigarettes and old clothing for eggs, vegetables, vino, pasta and the occasional scrawny chicken.

The continuous foul weather was not what we had expected Italy to produce. I wrote a friend in England:

> I hasten to disillusion you about the climate, but it must be the worst in the whole bloody world. It either burns the balls off you in summer, or freezes them off in winter. In between, it *rots* them off with endless rains. The only time I'm comfortable is in my sleeping bag, wearing woollen battledress and burrowed under half a dozen extra blankets. That's when we are in billets of course, such as the cellar I am now sharing with my batman and sometimes a pig or two that wanders in out of the stormy night. For most of the time recently we've been hiking in the mountains with only a cellophane gas cape to keep the elements at bay. The first travel agent I see back home with a poster of Sunny Italy in his window is going to get a damn big rock right through the glass.

Since the conditions under which we lived were much the same as those being endured by the natural inhabitants of Castropignano, shared adversity tended to dissolve whatever prejudices against the Italians still remained amongst us. These people, who had always lived on the hard edge of bare subsistence and who had now been made virtually destitute by war, did not whine and beg or bemoan their fate but carried on in a way that commanded respect and admiration from the Canadian *soldati,* many of whom had themselves known the acrid taste of poverty in "civvy street." I wrote:

I'm really amazed the way attitudes toward the Eyeties have changed. Before the war we were all taught to believe the Germans were such brave, clever, hardworking, God-fearing people, and the Italians were a bunch of cowardly, greasy good-for-nothings who waved their paws a lot, made plenty of noise, but wouldn't get their ass off the pot for love or money. Now it turns out *they're* the ones who are really the salt of the earth. The ordinary folk, that is. They have to work so hard to stay alive it's a wonder they aren't as sour as green lemons, but instead they're full of fun and laughter.

They're also tough as hell, and goddamn brave. A few weeks ago one old geezer showed up at BHQ with a big wicker hamper. We thought it was full of eggs to trade for cigs, but it was actually full of detonators from German Teller mines! The old character had watched the Jerries lay about a hundred mines in a mountain road and when they moved on he lifted every mine, took out the detonators, and brought the lot to us to prove the road was safe for us to travel. Didn't ask for anything in return either. In fact, he seemed to think it was a hell of a joke. But those things are often booby-trapped. He had more guts than me to tackle them on his own...

Nearly all the men and most of the officers have found Eyetie families of their own. We provide the grub and they find the vino and *Mamma Mia* does the cooking, and it's a ball. They ought to hate our guts nearly as much as Jerry's, but the only ones I wouldn't trust are the priests, lawyers, and the big shopkeepers, landowners and such. They were mostly all Fascists under Musso, and likely still are at heart. I doubt if many of the ordinary people ever were...

During our stay in Castropignano some of us were actually given leaves—the first since our departure from Scotland. Of its nearly nine hundred men, each infantry regiment in the division was permitted to send twenty-eight at a time on a two-day pass to Campobasso, which the staff had now grandiloquently renamed Canada Town.

... Only a dozen of the forty or so officers who landed on the beaches are still with us. The rest are dead or wounded or sick and invalided back to Canada or England. This week some of the survivors, including yours truly, got leave in recognition of long service. Al Park and I got a 48-hour leave to Canada Town. There we were able to luxuriate under a lukewarm shower, drink rotgut vino, watch a British Service concert that might have amused me when I was still in kindergarten, wander about in company with several hundred other bored *soldati* and, for sex, sit around and pull our puds. Hell's bloody balls! We can do all those things to better advantage and in a lot more comfort up in Castropigface! And it doesn't make things any better either to know the gilded (gelded?) lilies of the staff have mostly departed *from* Campobasso on extended leaves to the real flesh pots in Naples and Salerno. I hope like hell they all pick up a colossal dose!

One day late in November a friend invited me to accompany him on a visit to 3rd Brigade which was then laboriously scrabbling its way northward through the mountains toward the headwaters of the Sangro River where the Germans had anchored their so-called Bernhard Line.

As our jeep jounced over mountain trails, cratered, blown and generally savaged by the demolition experts of 1st

Paratroop Division, we encountered what for me was a new and singularly ugly aspect of war... refugees making their painful way southward.

Not before or since have I seen human beings who seemed so pitiable. We came upon them in little clots and clusters trudging along the roadsides through a veil of sleet. They were clad in unidentifiable scraps of black, rain-soaked clothing and many walked barefoot in coagulating mud that was barely above the freezing point. Shapeless bundles slung over their shoulders, they plodded by with downcast eyes, mute and expressionless. We noticed that there were no men of young or middle years among them. We were soon to find out why.

At 3rd Brigade Headquarters a grim West Nova Scotia Highlander lieutenant undertook to guide us deeper into an increasingly desolate landscape, and it was he who explained about the refugees.

"Before he pulled back, Jerry rounded up all the men and boys fit to work and took them to work on the fortifications along the Sangro. We've had a few escape into our lines. They tell us they get damn all to eat and are shot out of hand if they don't work hard enough, or try to escape. They're kept at it till they drop, then they're just left lying in the rain and snow to live or die on their own. But that's not the half of it! Nearly every village on our front has been systematically destroyed. Jerry took everything the people had in the way of food and livestock, then turfed them out, burned what would burn and blew everything else to hell. In one village the bastards blew down the church with women and kids sheltering inside...

"They herded most of the rest of the people off toward our lines warning them they'd be machine-gunned if they turned back. As you can see, we can't get wheeled transport up here except for jeeps, so they have to walk about ten miles to the rear, except for the sick or mothers with real young kids. We get them out on wheels somehow...

"Keep it under your hats, but our boys are so fucking well brassed off about it, they aren't taking any prisoners. Not those 1st Para bastards anyhow!"

Third Brigade had just occupied one of the demolished villages and we went forward to it on foot. The devastation was virtually total. Nothing remained except heaps of rubble but, despite the cold, the sickly stench of death proclaimed that not all the inhabitants had been able—or had been permitted—to escape. It was a revolting spectacle.

At the time, the Allied command appeared to have been very little disturbed by this barbarism. It was said that the Germans were simply pursuing the "scorched-earth" policy they had developed in Russia, where everything which might conceivably have been of any use to the Russian army was destroyed, and the civilian population—rendered homeless and destitute—was deliberately converted into a living obstacle in the path of the advancing Russian troops. Presumably because our brass hats considered the scorched-earth policy a legitimate military tactic, the atrocities inflicted on the Italian peasants in the Sangro mountains rated no more than a few casual and non-condemnatory references even in the official military histories written after the war.

In fact, those isolated little clusters of stone hovels clinging precariously to their inhospitable eyries in a remote backwater were not, could never have been, of the slightest military significance to anyone. The truth of the matter was that nearly a dozen hill villages were deliberately and savagely reduced to rubble as an act of reprisal for an attack which some Italian partisans made on the paratroopers.

I heard the story first from Riccardo Sacconi, a resident of Campobasso, during a visit in 1953. He told me the partisans—there were only five of them—had ambushed a German supply convoy near the hill village of San Pietro. They managed to set one or two trucks on fire but, unfortunately for them, a second convoy carrying a company of paratroopers arrived on the scene a few minutes later. The fight that followed was fierce, but when it was over all the partisans were dead.

Next day the Germans began reprisals in a classic example of the Teutonic terror—the *furor Germanicus*—which was visited on almost every country the Germans occupied during World War II but which, except insofar as it affected the Jews, we have largely chosen to forget now that the Germans have become our valued allies.

It will not so easily be expunged from the memories of those who still dwell in the bleak ranges where the Sangro takes its birth. And if I were among the hordes of wealthy German tourists who overrun Italy each summer, this is one region I would take pains to avoid.

Having heard and verified the story from other sources, I tried to discover the identity of the partisans, but this no one could tell me. All that was known was that five mutilated bodies were dumped down in the tiny town square of San Pietro before an enforced audience consisting of all the townsfolk including the youngest children. Then the Germans doused the corpses with gasoline and incinerated them; and so they vanished out of memory.

But I remember Giovanni, and I wonder.

PART IV

Still wept the rain, roared guns,

Still swooped into the swamps of flesh and blood,

All to the drabness of uncreation sunk,

And all thought dwindled to a moan...

EDMUND BLUNDEN "THIRD YPRES"

BECAUSE OF THE CONDITIONS under which we had been existing for so many weeks, disease had taken a heavy toll. Epidemic jaundice in particular caused many casualties. Among its victims, all evacuated to North Africa, were Alex Campbell and John Tweedsmuir. Both went unwillingly (Alex had to be ordered into hospital) and both were sorely missed. With Tweedsmuir's departure, Ack Ack Kennedy again took over as commanding officer.

On November 25 Kennedy and I attended a divisional briefing in Campobasso. A fiery brigadier from Eighth Army Headquarters, backed by an immense map, gave us "the form" from the stage of a warm and well-lit theatre.

"As you may have guessed, gentlemen, our objective remains Rome. Can't let the Hun spend the rest of the winter there all nice and comfy-cosy. So we shall jolly well turf him out. Over on the left... here... the Yanks will burst through the Bernhard Line and streak up the Liri Valley past Cassino and pop into Rome from the south. Our chaps... over here... will smash across the Sangro and gallop up the coast to Pescara, then make a left hook into the mountains and pounce on Rome from the east. Our part of the show will open with a colossal crack at the mouth of the Sangro River... 1st Canadian Division will spearhead the advance after the breakthrough has been made. We've bags of tanks and guns so it should be plain sailing, what?"

There are some phrases which can chill the veteran soldier's blood more effectively than any polar blizzard—and "spearhead the advance" is one such. Kennedy and I had nothing much to say to one another as our open jeep jounced back to Castropigface through driving sleet. There was no joy in me as I contemplated the prospects. There was even less joy when, two days later, I accompanied Kennedy on reconnaissance, prior to moving the battalion to the Adriatic coast.

Winter had preceded us. The snow that had been steadily building on the inland peaks had been falling just as heavily into the grey valleys of the coastal plains, but melting as it fell. The *torrentes* were bearing eloquent witness to their name, racing and roaring to the sea. Heavy with saffron-coloured muck, they sucked at the shaking supports of the prefabricated Bailey spans with which our sappers had replaced the demolished Italian bridges. From the distant coast of Yugoslavia the infamous *bora* gale drove black clouds in from seaward almost at ground level, enveloping the wetlands in dark and deathly mist. Everything that was not solid rock seemed to be turning fluid. Lines of olive trees gnarled by a hundred winters stood gaunt as gibbets on dripping ridges above vineyards that had become slimy swamps. In the villages the sad stone houses seemed to have shrunk even closer to one another under the burden of unrelenting rain and sleet.

It was a time for plants to die, for birds to flee, for small animals to burrow deep into the earth, and for human beings to huddle by charcoal braziers and wait the winter out. It was assuredly neither the time nor place for waging war.

Kennedy's disgusted comment as we headed back to rejoin the Regiment was prophetic.

"*Gallop* up the coast to Pescara, will we? Gallop like a goddamn snail more like!"

The first day of December, 1943, found a great convoy of trucks rolling eastward out of the mountains carrying 1st Division toward the visceral rumble of a singularly savage battle which had then been in progress for three days as two British and one Indian Division delivered the "colossal crack" against the Bernhard Line. The Sangro was crossed and a bridgehead established, but at fearsome cost. A liaison officer from the British 78th Division told me about it with tears— not of sorrow, but of rage—in his eyes.

"We've had five hundred casualties crossing this one flaming river! And for what? Haven't any of the high mucky-mucks looked at their frigging maps? There'll be half a dozen Sangros before we get to Pescara ... *if* we get to Pescara. Thank God you're taking over, Canada. We've *had* this show!"

The coastal plain north of the Sangro is a narrow shelf between the towering Maiella Mountains and the sea. At intervals of a mile or so, it is deeply gashed from mountains to tidewater by steep-sided ravines and river valleys. In summertime this constrained ribbon of lowland presents a singularly formidable obstacle to an attacking army. Once the winter floods have set in, it becomes almost impassable.

If our high command seemed blind to the nature of the ground and its defensive possibilities, the German staff was not. Even while the Bernhard Line was being breached, the Germans were preparing a new line along the Moro River, a scant nine miles north of the Sangro. And they had already manned it with fresh troops, including another of their more famous formations, the 90th Light Panzer-Grenadier Division which also had been part of Rommel's army.

By the morning of December 5, 78th Division's Royal Irish Fusiliers had reached the near bank of the Moro. That afternoon we were ordered to relieve them and become the "spearhead of the advance."

It was pelting rain when I went forward with the Fusiliers' intelligence officer to see what he could show me. Long files of soaked and muddy Fusiliers wound their way past us, moving to the rear. Their faces were as colourless as paper pulp and they were so exhausted they hardly seemed to notice the intense shelling the coastal road was getting as they straggled down it.

But *I* noticed, as I never had before. The rancid taint of cordite seemed to work on me like some powerful and alien drug. My heart was thumping to no regular rhythm. It was hard to draw breath, and I was shivering spasmodically though I was not cold. Worst of all, I had to wrestle with an almost irresistible compulsion to stop, to turn about, to join those deathly visaged men who were escaping from the battle that awaited me.

I paused, fumbled for a cigarette and offered one to the Irish lieutenant trudging at my side. He lit a match and held it in cupped hands for me... but I turned my face away, for in that instant I realized what was happening to me. I was sickening with the most virulent and deadly of all apprehensions... the fear of fear itself.

At length the Irishman and I reached the edge of the plateau forming the south wall of the valley. We lay on our bellies behind some dripping bushes and I raised my binoculars and hid my face behind them. There was nothing to see through the haze of rain and mist.

"'Fraid there's not much I can show you." The voice of the man beside me was strained, almost impatient. "Been thick as soup ever since we got here so we've not seen what the far bank looks like, and my chaps were too done in to go patrolling. Just the same, you can stake your soul old Jerry's over there, and good and ready, I'll be bound."

"Well," he added when I did not reply, "nothing more I can do here, eh? Best be catching up to my regiment. Cheer-oh... and best of luck."

He scrambled to his feet and vanished into the rain scud with what seemed like indecent haste. I had an almost overwhelming urge to run after him, but fought it down. High-flying shells droned their dirge overhead while I lay on the wet earth, trying to pull myself together.

It was almost dusk when I reached BHQ, which was in a *casa* half a mile south of the river mouth. Kennedy was fuming with impatience.

"Where the hell have *you* been? Goddamn it, we're to cross the Moro right away. No preparation. No support. What've you found out?"

"Sorry, sir, not much. The Irish couldn't tell me anything and there's nothing to be seen from our side of the valley."

He grunted angrily.

"Can you get scouts out there and find a crossing place? And get them back inside an hour?"

"Don't know, sir. I can try."

"Try? Goddamn you, *do it!"*

Oh Christ, I thought, I'll have to go myself... I'll have to go... No!... I'll send Langstaff... He's far the best man for the job... I'll send him out...

The scouts were brewing tea in a nearby cow byre. They watched me without expression as I briefed George Langstaff and two other men. They knew I had at least glimpsed the valley in daylight and so was the logical one to lead the patrol. What they did not know was that the mere prospect of descending into that ominously shrouded valley was paralyzing me. I was convinced that death or ghastly mutilation awaited me there. The certainty was absolute! The Worm that was growing in my gut had told me so.

Four months earlier I would have welcomed the chance to make a patrol like this. Two months past and I would have accepted it as a risky job that had to be done. But on this December day I would have given everything I was, or ever hoped to be, for a way out.

There was none.

I took the patrol out ... and nothing happened. The Worm had lied. The darkness was so opaque and the whip of wind and rain so masked our movements that we went and returned unseen and unmolested. We felt our way to the swollen river and waded along its overflowing banks until we found a ford. And we got back to our own lines just in time for Langstaff to become guide for Able Company as it moved into the attack.

After wading the river at the ford, Able, with my old platoon in the lead, had barely begun to climb the far bank when twenty or thirty German machine guns began stitching the darkness with vicious needles of tracer. Flares—some green, some red—burst overhead, and these sos signals were instantly answered by the distant grumble of enemy guns. Within seconds roaring salvos of artillery and mortar shells were falling on Able Company, the explosions illuminating the bleak valley floor with fluctuating and hellish flames.

I was with Kennedy on the south escarpment when the Germans opened up, and we were appalled by the ferocity of the German reaction. After only a few minutes Kennedy yelled to the signaller manning the radio to call Able back.

As the survivors came straggling out of that inferno, we realized we had never before seen war in its full and dreadful magnitude. Seven Platoon in particular had suffered fearfully. The platoon commander who had succeeded me had been severely wounded, and Sergeant Bates and several other men I had known and led were dead or dying.

All through the rest of that long, wet night the forward troops manned their weapons while all of us tried to avoid thoughts of the morrow. At dawn we heard that 2nd Brigade had attacked at San Leonardo four miles upstream, and had also been bloodily repulsed.

Shortly thereafter we received orders to force a crossing on our front at whatever cost.

THE BATTLE THAT followed began at 1400 hours on December 6 and ended on December 15, barely a mile north of where it had begun. It was a ten-day blood bath that cost the Regiment over a hundred and fifty battle casualties.

The opening attack was made in broad daylight by Charley Company under cover of the strongest artillery support Division could muster. It was a devastating barrage... but the enemy replied with equal violence and within minutes

Charley was being pounded into the saturated valley floor under a titanic upheaval of mud and steel. Dog, coming up behind, tried to avoid the worst of that holocaust and swung to the left into a smoke screen being laid by our own heavy mortars, and the entire company simply vanished from our ken. When, after nearly an hour, there was still no word from Dog, Kennedy became so distraught that he ordered me and a Battalion Headquarters runner to follow, then flung himself hell-bent down the slope.

My whole being screamed resistance. Three times we were pinned, grovelling in the mud, before we reached the river and struggled through its icy waters. On the far shore we fell into a slimy ditch with the survivors of one of Charley Company's platoons. We tried to find out from them what was happening, but nobody knew. The German counter-barrage had by then become so heavy that platoons and even sections were isolated and out of communication with one another, cowering in the muck as almost continuous explosions leapt about them.

Kennedy led us on in search of Charley Company Head-quarters, and we miraculously stumbled on it in a tiny cave at the foot of a steep cliff; but the company commander was missing and a terrified sergeant could tell us nothing. Kennedy realized the situation was hopeless and that we would have to withdraw, but he had no way of issuing the necessary order until he could get to his radio. So he led us back across the valley.

My memory of that return must be akin to what a drowning man feels during the endless, agonizing moments when he is sinking slowly into the depths. My chest felt crushed and I was gasping for air by the time we reached the road which climbed the south slope. There must have been a lull in the shelling then or else Kennedy was just so anxious to reach the radio that he did not care what the enemy might do, for he led us straight up the road in full view of the Germans opposite. We had not gone fifty feet when they bracketed us with a salvo of Eighty-eights.

Something struck my right foot a numbing blow and a stunning concussion flung me face down into the mud. I heard screaming close at hand and, struggling to my knees, saw Kennedy on his knees in the centre of the smoking road, shaking his head slowly from side to side like an old and tired dog, but the screaming was not his. Ten feet behind him the runner, a young lad whose name I never knew, was humping jerkily away from his own leg which had been severed at the thigh. In the instant that I saw him, he gave one final bubbling shriek, collapsed, and mercifully was still.

I heard Kennedy's voice as from some distant mountain peak.

"Get up, Mowat! Goddamn you! *Up!*"

He was standing over me, swaying, but apparently unhurt.

"Can't," I said quite calmly. "Hit in the leg, I think."

In a moment he had me by the shoulders and hoisted me to my feet. We stumbled over the crest and fell into the cover of a gully as another salvo of Eighty-eights ploughed into the road behind us.

There was no pain in my foot and glorious euphoria was overwhelming me. *I had a Blighty!* Soon I would be on my way back down the line to a field hospital and then perhaps still farther back for a sea voyage to England or even Canada! The sound and fury... and the fear... would be behind me. But somewhere within my skull a spiteful voice poured vitriol on my joy. "Coward!" it said. "You gutless wonder!"

A couple of men from Baker Company spotted us and now they helped me to the regimental aid post which the medical officer, Captain Charlie Krakauer, had pushed forward to the doubtful shelter of a ruined hovel on the very lip of the valley. Kennedy was in a desperate hurry to get on to BHQ but he spared a moment for me.

"Good lad, Squib. You've done okay."

I gave him a lying grin but I was thinking, Thank Christ I'm getting out of here!

Someone helped me onto a stretcher in the dim-lit room and Krakauer was soon bending over my feet. I heard him grunt and felt a tug, then his face was above me, split by a lopsided grin.

"You lucky little prick! Shell cut your boot open from end to end and hardly creased the skin. Wait till we get a Band-Aid on it and you can go right back to work!"

I did not believe him! Outraged, I rolled over and sat up... and shrieked as a flame of agony seared deep into my backside. Krakauer's smile faded as with one big hand he pushed me back on the stretcher and rolled me over. Again I heard him grunt as he swiftly scissored off the seat of my trousers... then a bellow of raucous laughter burst from him.

It must have been the last laughter heard at the regimental aid post that day and for days thereafter. It was justified. Sticking out of the right cheek of my ass, unnoticed until I sat upon it, was a wedge of steel shell casing which had penetrated to a depth of perhaps half an inch. Charlie yanked it out with his fingers and presented it to me with a flourish.

"Keep this in memory of me," he said.

I departed limping slightly, for feeling had not yet returned to my foot, and with the seat of my pants held together with a large safety pin contributed by a stretcher-bearer. I was not on my way to Blighty. My destination was rear BHQ, there to seek out a new pair of boots and a whole pair of trousers. I also had some hopes of being able to hide for awhile in the relatively shellproof gully where rear headquarters was located, but even this was not to be.

I was met by a white-faced and fluttering Jimmy Bird who told me Kennedy had been unable to contact Dog Company on the radio and had therefore decided the attack would have to be renewed in order to rescue Dog. Charley Company, whose survivors had mostly dribbled back by now, was in no shape for another round; so I was to fetch what was left of Able and lead it up to take part in a new attack in company with Baker.

There was no time to change either boots or trousers. Physically sickened by the mere thought of going back into the valley, I stumbled down the road to Able's area where I found Alex's replacement, a newly arrived captain whom I did not know, and gave him my message. He hardly seemed to hear.

Al Park was standing nearby, a strange, obdurate look on his face, and his eyes hooded. He beckoned me off to one side.

"Paddy's bought it," he said in a voice thin with grief or rage—I could not tell which. "Phosphorous grenade exploded in his face and burned him to a crisp... died in the ambulance on the way out. We just now heard... the company's down to about forty bods still able to pull a trigger. God almighty, Squib, they can't send us back in now!"

Yes, I thought dully, they can. They will. But I said nothing, and Al's gaze dropped from my face to the mud at our feet. Memory flickered and I saw Paddy kneeling beside the dead

Italian officer on that dusty road in Sicily. The Irish Rover...
gone now for good.

Al uncorked his water bottle and offered it to me. We both
took choking gulps of the straight issue rum. It did not restore
my failing courage but at least it helped a little to deaden the
throbbing fear.

Kennedy was waiting for us near the aid post, which was
now clustered about with jeep ambulances taking out the
wounded from Charley Company. Moments later we were
descending into the void again.

The German fire, which had slackened somewhat after
Charley's withdrawal, started up anew and, so it seemed, with
redoubled weight and fury. Most of the artillery of the German
Corps holding the coast section, augmented by self-propelled
guns and an avalanche of mortar bombs and rocket projectiles,
was now concentrated in the valley. However, the very mas-
siveness of the bombardment served to partially defeat its purpose. It would not permit us to retreat. We had no choice but
to stampede forward up the enemy-held slopes, for there alone
could we hope to find shelter from the annihilating blast.

I have no recollection of that second crossing until I found
myself in the same little cave that had been Charley Company's Headquarters during their ill-fated attack, and being
roundly cursed by the battalion signals sergeant who did not
recognize me in my mud-caked state and thought I was one of
his signallers. Then Kennedy appeared, wild-eyed and glaring
like a maniac.

"Jerry's on the run!" he cried. "But the goddamn radio's
gone out! Mowat! Go back and get what's left of Charley!"

Of *that* crossing of the Moro I have no memories at all.
Darkness had fallen by the time I returned to Kennedy again.

By that time a few men from Able and Baker had thrust forward to the edge of the northern plateau, where German tanks and a savage infantry counterattack forced them to dig in.

What followed was the kind of night men dream about in afteryears, waking in a cold sweat to a surge of gratitude that it is but a dream. It was a delirium of sustained violence. Small pockets of Germans that had been cut off throughout our bridgehead fired their automatic weapons in hysterical dismay at every shadow. The grind of enemy tanks and self-propelled guns working their way along the crest was multiplied by echoes until it sounded like an entire Panzer army. Illuminating flares flamed in darkness with a sick radiance. The snap and scream of high-velocity tank shells pierced the brutal guttural of an endless cannonade from both German and Canadian artillery. Moaning Minnie projectiles whumped down like thunderbolts, searching for our hurriedly dug foxholes. Soldiers of both sides, blundering through the vineyards, fired with panicky impartiality in all directions. And it began to rain again, a bitter, penetrating winter rain.

December 7 dawned overcast and brought black news. The engorged Sangro River had risen twenty feet in as many hours and washed away the precious pontoon bridges, leaving 1st and 2nd brigades isolated from the rest of the army. Worse still, the Germans had smashed a bridgehead which had been established across the Moro at grim cost by 2nd Brigade near San Leonardo, leaving us holding the sole remaining foothold on the northern bank.

As icy rain squalls swept the smoking valley, things grew worse. A troop of British tanks attempting to cross in our support became hopelessly bogged and were picked off, one by one, by German self-propelled guns. Then came word that despite our success at the mouth of the river, the divisional commander intended to persist with the bloody attempts to make a main crossing at San Leonardo. Therefore, we were not to be reinforced, and much of the artillery support which had been vitally instrumental to our survival was to be switched to the San Leonardo sector. Left on our own, our orders were to "engage the enemy closely" in order to draw his attention away from 2nd Brigade's assault.

This order was superfluous, for the Germans now proceeded to engage *us* as closely as they could.

During the next thirty-six hours eleven separate counterattacks were flung against us. Yet somehow we clung to our precarious salient across the Moro, and by drawing upon ourselves the German fire and reinforcements, including a fresh regiment from the 1st Paratroop Division, enabled our sister brigade to make a new crossing of the river at San Leonardo and consolidate a bridgehead there.

The cost had been appalling. When the firing died down on our sector, stretcher and burial parties scouring the slimy slopes and the tangles of shell-torn debris found one hundred and seventy German corpses. Our own dead and wounded amounted to a third of the four hundred or so Hasty Pees who had gone into the valley of the shadow.

FOR ME THE Moro is to be remembered as the lair of the Worm That Never Dies—and of one particular victim. He was a stretcher-bearer, an older man—he might have been all of thirty-five—who had been with the Regiment since the autumn of 1939.

By day and by night the bearers had to make their way across the valley, crawling forward to the lead platoon positions, if necessary. Some of them must have made that agonizing passage a score of times. For them there was no rest and no surcease; no burrowing in a slit trench to escape the sound and fury. For them there was only a journey into the inferno, then the withdrawal to momentary sanctuary, and the return to hell once more.

That was the hardest thing to bear. Those who remained under sustained and unremitting fire could partially armour themselves with the apathy of the half-dead; but those who had to come and go, knowing the searing repetition of brief escape followed by a new immersion in the bath of terror— those were the ones who paid the heaviest price.

On the last night of our ordeal I was descending the north slope, numbed and passionless, drugged with fatigue, dead on my feet, when I heard someone singing! It was a rough voice, husky yet powerful. A cluster of mortar bombs came crashing down and I threw myself into the mud. When I could hear again, the first sound that came to me was the singing voice. Cautiously I raised myself just as a starshell burst overhead, and saw him coming toward me through that blasted wasteland.

Stark naked, he was striding through the cordite stench with his head held high and his arms swinging. His body shone white in the brilliant light of the flare, except for what appeared to be a glistening crimson sash that ran from one shoulder down one thigh and dripped from his lifted foot.

He was singing "Home on the Range" at the top of his lungs.

The Worm That Never Dies had taken him.

SECURING THE MORO bridgehead brought us no respite. Until December 19 we remained in action, first defending what we had taken, then breaking out in an attempt to drive the paratroopers back toward the ramparts of Ortona which we could now see encrusting a blunt promontory jutting into the leaden waters of the Adriatic. Ambulance jeeps were perpetually on the move, weaving their way along cratered tracks back and forth across the devastated valley through a desultory fall of shells. For the most part they were laden with men who could have served as illustrations for a macabre catalogue of the infinite varieties of mutilation; but for the first time since we had gone to war they also carried casualties who bore no visible wounds.

These were the victims of what was officially termed "battle fatigue"—"shell shock" they called it in the First World War. Both descriptions were evasive euphemisms. The military mind will not, perhaps does not dare, admit that there comes a time to every fighting man (unless death or bloody ruination of the flesh forestalls it) when the Worm—not steel and flame—becomes his nemesis.

My father had warned me of this in a letter I received just before we left Castropignano for the Adriatic sector. It was a letter so unlike his usual robust and cheerful chronicles of trivia at home that I can believe it was dictated by the Celtic prescience which he claimed as part of his inheritance.

Keep it in mind during the days ahead that war does inexplicable things to people, and no man can guess how it is going to affect him until he has had a really stiff dose of it ... The most unfortunate ones after any war are not those with missing limbs; they are the ones who have had their spiritual feet knocked out from under them. The beer halls and gutters are still full of such poor bastards from my war, and nobody understands or cares what happened to them... I remember two striking examples from my old Company in the 4th Battalion. Both damn fine fellows, yet both committed suicide in the Line. They did not shoot themselves—they let the Germans do it because they had reached the end of the tether. But they never knew what was the matter with them; that they had become empty husks, were spiritually depleted, were burned out.

My own understanding of the nature of the Worm, and of the inexorable way it liquefies and then consumes the inner substance of its victims, was chillingly enlarged on the day we broke out of our bridgehead.

Baker Company led the breakout and fought its way for nearly a mile along the coastal road leading toward Ortona before being halted by flanking fire from the far lip of a ravine to the left of the road. Kennedy took me with him and went forward to assess the situation, and we got well mortared for our pains. The Germans overlooked and dominated our line of advance to such a degree that we could not push past until they were driven off. We assumed that a unit of 3rd Brigade, which was supposed to be advancing on our flank, would take care of this and so we dug in to await events.

We had not long to wait. Still anxious to divert attention from his main thrust out of San Leonardo and unwilling to reinforce the coastal sector, the divisional commander passed the word that we must take out the enemy position ourselves.

Furthermore, we were ordered to attack immediately and in such a way that "the enemy will conclude you are the spearhead of the main assault." Once again we were to be the goat in the tiger hunt.

From an observation post my section had hurriedly established in the dubious shelter of a collapsed shed, I looked out over a sea of mud dotted here and there with the foundered hulks of shell-shattered farm buildings and strewn with flotsam of broken vineyard posts and twisted skeins of vineyard wire. It was a scene of mind-wrenching desolation, one that seemed doubly ominous beneath the lowering winter sky.

It also seemed grimly lifeless... except... something was moving near a ravaged ruin on the valley floor. I focussed my binoculars... stared hard... and wished I hadn't. Looming large in the circle of my lenses were two huge sows gorging themselves on the swollen corpse of a mule. I knew they would as greedily stuff their gravid bellies with human meat if chance afforded... and I knew the chance would certainly be afforded—all too soon.

The battle we were about to enter promised nothing but disaster—a frontal attack in daylight over open ground, in full view of determined paratroopers manning prepared and fortified positions and well supported by heavy weapons. Only a massive weight of accompanying armour could have given an infantry attack the ghost of a chance, and we had only a troop—three tanks—in support. Furthermore, it was obvious to all of us, tankers and infantrymen alike, that neither wheels *nor* tracks could move far through the morass of mud in the bottom of the valley.

Shortly before the attack was due to begin, Kennedy, to my belly-quivering dismay, detailed me to accompany the tanks *on foot,* in order to provide liaison between them and the infantry should radio communication fail.

Zero hour came at 1600. There was a brief outpouring of artillery shells and heavy mortar bombs from our supporting guns; and as the far side of the gully began to be obscured by muddy geysers, flame and smoke, the men of Dog Company started down the slope.

I watched them go from behind the protection of the troop commander's tank, terrified on their behalf and on my own as well. Not more than fifty men remained to the company, an insignificant and pathetically vulnerable handful, thinly dispersed across that funereal waste of mud and wreckage.

As was intended, the Germans did not suspect this attack was only a diversion; and since it seemed to directly threaten Ortona, the coastal anchor of their new defence line, they reacted by flinging everything they had at us. Dog Company and the valley floor itself disappeared under the smoke and fumes of the most concentrated bombardment I had yet seen.

As the enemy barrage thundered up the slope, I plastered myself against the back of the troop commander's Sherman, desperately wishing I was inside its armoured carapace. The din was so tremendous I did not even hear the roar of accelerating engines and, before I knew what was happening, all three tanks were lurching away from me.

Because the Shermans were tightly "buttoned up"—all hatches closed and dogged—the troop commander had been unable to let me know he had received an urgent call for help from Dog. The remnants of that company, having somehow succeeded in reaching the far side of the valley, had been pinned down by machine-gun fire hosing into them from several bunkers which were impervious to anything except point-blank shelling from tank guns. Fully aware of the odds against them, the tankers were gamely attempting to respond to Dog's SOS.

With their abrupt departure I was left nakedly exposed to the tempest of explosions. Wildly I looked about for shelter, but the nearest was a shattered house two hundred yards away, from which I knew Kennedy was watching the battle. I could not go there. There seemed nothing else for it but to fling myself in pursuit of the tanks, impelled by a primal need to interpose their armoured bulk between me and the apocalyptic fury of the German guns.

Reaching the bottom of the slope, the Shermans encountered a maze of drainage ditches in which one of them immediately got itself bogged while the other two, slewing helplessly in deepening slime, dared go no farther. I reached the mired tank in a lung-bursting sprint and, so consuming was my need to escape the cataclysmic bombardment, I began beating on its steel flanks with my fists while howling to be taken in.

My voice was lost even to my own ears in a bellowing drumfire of shell bursts. The Germans had spotted the tanks and were now bent on annihilating them. Bombs, shells and streams of machine-gun bullets converged on the Shermans. The sound and fury rose to a level beyond my powers of description . . . and beyond the limits of my endurance.

Reason abandoned me. I dropped to my belly and, heedless of what must have happened if the bogged tank had attempted to move, tried to burrow under it, between its tracks. But it had already sunk so deeply into the mire that I could not force my way beneath it. There was no place there to hide.

Then an armour-piercing shell struck the Sherman. I did not hear it hit but felt the massive machine jolt under the impact, and at once my lungs began to fill with raw petrol fumes.

Somewhere inside myself there was a shriek of agony, for I could already feel the searing heat that would engulf me as the tank flamed into a livid torch. It did not happen. There was no brew-up—but that I did not know, for I was already in full flight up the slope, churning through the muck like some insensate robot. A salvo of heavy stuff dropped close enough to slap me flat on my face under a living wall of mud. But the robot got to its feet and staggered on.

I did not pause at the ruins where Kennedy was sheltering. Reaching the shell-pocked road I trotted along at a steady, purposeful lope. God alone knows how far I might have run—perhaps until exhaustion felled me—had I not been intercepted by Franky Hammond, commander of our anti-tank platoon, who was trying to get forward with one of his 6-pounder guns. He caught my arm as I trotted sightlessly past his halted jeep and spun me up against the little vehicle. Then he shook me until I went limp.

"Drink this!" he ordered, and thrust the neck of his rum-filled water bottle into my mouth.

Then, "Get in the jeep! Now show me the way to BHQ."

Franky had saved me from the Worm.

When, a few minutes later, I reported to Kennedy that I had lost contact with the tanks and with Dog Company as well, he seemed too preoccupied to care. Having heard that Dog Company's commander and his entire headquarters group had been wiped out and two of the three platoon commanders had been killed or badly wounded, Kennedy had immediately radioed Brigade for permission to call off the attack. Brigade had replied that, under orders from Division, *we were to renew the battle and keep on renewing it until told to stop.*

I did not remain to witness the ensuing debacle as Able Company was put into the meat grinder. Kennedy sent me back across the Moro in Hammond's jeep on some now-forgotten errand to rear BHQ which by then was out of range of most of the German guns. Presumably I did whatever it was I had been told to do, after which our quartermaster, George Hepburn, found me wandering aimlessly about and took me into his snug retreat in the cellar of an undamaged house where he plied me with rum until I passed out.

When I woke next morning it was to find a worried Doc Macdonald standing over me with a mug of tea in his hand.

"Jeez, boss, I figured you for a goner. You was yellin' and whoopin' like a bunch o' chimpanzees the whole damn night. You gotta take it easy with that issue hooch."

THE BUTCHERY in the gully lasted for three days and ended only when units of 3rd Brigade, finally breaking out of the San Leonardo positions, came up on our left flank. The Regiment had done what it had been told to do.

On December 19, when we were pulled out of the coastal salient after two weeks of continuous battle, we believed we would be asked to do no more, at least until we had been given time to rest and lick our wounds. Secure in this supposition, we slouched off to a staging area in an olive grove near San Leonardo where we at once began improvising shelters against a frigid downpour. The miserable circumstances did not bother us. We would have been content to bivouac on the frozen tundra of Siberia, so long as we knew we would be left alone for a healing time.

My state of mind is reflected in a letter I wrote on the first day at San Leonardo.

> I have been neglecting you and everyone else on a grand scale recently and may have to do so for awhile longer, though I hope to God it doesn't work out that way. It isn't so much the lack of time to write as it is the lack of will. What have I got to say, anyway? I could tell you I was having a hell of a good time shooting and being shot at, but you would read the lie in that. I could try to tell you how I really feel deep down inside, but that wouldn't do either of us any ruddy good. The damnable truth is we are in really different worlds, on totally different planes, and I don't *know* you anymore, I only know the you that was. I wish I could explain the desperate sense of isolation, of not belonging to my own past, of being adrift in some kind of alien space. It is one of the toughest things we have to bear—that and the primal, gut-rotting worm of fear.
>
> Things have changed so much since Sicily. Too many pals gone West. Too many things that go wump in the night. The long claw of the Seapuss getting closer all the time. Too difficult trying to find the sense and meaning in any of this... Pray God we get a decent break. We need it worse than you could ever know...

During the morning of December 22 the sun broke thinly through the driven scud of another *bora* gale and men reacted like plants beginning to unfold after a too-long night. Groups gathered around the cook trucks for a mug of tea. As the wan sun fell upon us, there were even jokes about "only three more shooting days to Christmas." And there was hopeful talk of a possible mail distribution and of parcels from home. It was a time to think about presents.

One came to us.

Just before noon a single 8-inch shell from a long-range German gun came snoring overhead to bury itself in the centre of the bivouac area.

The explosion seemed of unprecedented violence. I was standing some distance from the burst and as the concussion buffeted me I saw a massive cone of mud spring full blown, like an instant genie, out of the sodden ground. A hot wind filled my nostrils. Childlike I screwed my eyes tight shut against this terror and willed my body not to run.

When I looked out into the world again it was to see a black-rimmed crater where the regimental aid post had stood short seconds earlier. There remained only some meaningless fragments of the equipment which, alone in war's panoply, is intended to heal rather than to destroy. There remained only bloodied fragments of Charlie Krakauer, of the medical sergeant and half a dozen orderlies and stretcher-bearers.

And yet this ghastly gift was but a token of Christmas still to come.

THE SLAUGHTERHOUSE MESS around the aid post was still being cleaned away when Kennedy was summoned to attend a Brigade O-group. As usual I accompanied him—but with a stone-cold heart. When we returned to the grove our own O-group was waiting for us. Al Park, now second-in-command of the remnant of Able Company, came over and took me by the arm. His long, white face was stiff with strain, and his eyes dark with anxiety.

"What's the word, Squib? Are we going into reserve?"

"No bloody fear," I told him in a voice taut with anger. "We've got another date with the *Tedeschi*."

He nodded; then for a moment his expression softened and I had a glimpse of the youngster I had known in Scotland.

"Ah well, what the hell? Who wants to make old bones? See you in Valhalla, chum."

The sun was gone and a cold mist was settling over the semi-circle of silent officers waiting tensely under a tree to hear their orders. Second Brigade, Kennedy told them, had managed to claw its way into the outskirts of Ortona but the street fighting which had then erupted had bogged them down in a bloody stalemate with the paratroopers. Therefore, 1st Brigade would go back into the line, and the Regiment would lead a sweeping left hook around Ortona in an attempt to force the Germans to abandon the town. We were then to "burst out and engage in," Kennedy gave us a wry grin, "fluid warfare to open up the front."

He did not tell his officers what the Brigade Intelligence Officer had told me: "Monty blew into Div HQ last night and he was frothing at the mouth. Passed the word to get on with it at any cost. The General told him the Div is worn down to the nub and ought to be relieved, but there ain't no reserves, so no reliefs. It's carry on, boys, and do or die, and bring me Pescara on a bleeding silver plate!"

THE ATTACK WENT in next morning behind a massive rolling barrage fired by five artillery regiments. Crouched in an unroofed barn which was serving as advanced Battalion Headquarters, I felt the reverberations of those hundreds of bursting shells as an obbligato to the unsteady pounding of my heart. I thought of my friends in Able and Baker companies leading the battalion into that throbbing void, and my guts contracted with mingled rage and fear.

For a time things went well enough, then both lead companies found themselves pinned down under machine-gun fire and the enemy counter-barrage just short of their objectives. The company commanders reported heavy casualties and Kennedy, as was his habit (one that I dreaded and abhorred), decided to go forward and see for himself what was happening. He beckoned me to follow.

The storm clouds rolling overhead seemed close enough to touch, and the land lay under a leaden obscurity drained of all colour and devoid of shape. Ankle-deep in sucking muck we plodded across a patchwork of little fields and vineyards. The explosions of our own and German shells pounded hideously inside my skull, yet Kennedy seemed unaware. Not once did he dive for cover or even so much as hunch his shoulders when the grating scream of an incoming projectile warned of imminent destruction. Senseless anger boiled up in the quaking bog within me: You goddamn pigheaded idiot! I mouthed in silence. What in hell are you trying to prove? Rage mounted—and sustained me.

A salvo of medium shells plunging through the overcast into the mud a few yards to our flank sent me grovelling. When I raised my head Kennedy was a dim shape in a dimmed world, plodding steadily onward. I scrambled to my feet, shouting aloud now, against the Doomsday roar:

"You crazy bastard!"

But still I followed him. I could not break the leash. More than this: When we eventually stumbled into what was left of Charley Company and Kennedy told me to go and find a squadron of Shermans which was supposed to be coming up in support on our right flank, I went without demur, though raging inwardly. *"The bastard's out to get me killed—get us all killed! Well, let him try!"*

False fury... but it kept the Worm at bay.

The axis of our attack was along a ridge dotted with farm buildings and dissected by countless drainage ditches. I made my way to the right and to the rear in a series of abrupt dashes from ditch to ditch, taking a swig of rum from my water bottle as I lay gasping in momentary shelter at the conclusion of each dash. Rum served to fuel my rage.

One such dash took me close to a hut whose partly collapsed stone walls still seemed capable of providing some protection, and the banshee screech of Moaning Minnie rockets sent me scuttling frantically toward this ruin. I reached it just as the bombs exploded a few score yards away. The blast flung me through the empty doorway with such violence that I sprawled full-length on top of a prone human figure who emitted a horrid gurgling belch. It was an unconscious protest, for he and two of his three companions—grey-clad paratroopers—were dead, their bodies mired in the muck and goat manure on the floor. The fourth man—dimly seen in that dim place—was sitting upright in a corner of the little unroofed room and his eyes met mine as I struggled to my hands and knees.

In that instant I was so convinced that this was death—that he would shoot me where I knelt—that I did not even try to reach for the carbine slung across my back. I remained transfixed for what seemed an interminable time, then in an unconscious reflex effort I flung myself sideways and rolled to my feet. I was lurching through the doorway when his thin voice reached me.

"Vasser... haff... you... vasser?"

I checked my rush and swung up against the outer wall, knowing then that I was safe, that he posed no threat. And I felt an inexplicable sense of recognition, almost as if I had heard his voice before. Cautiously I peered back through the doorway.

His left hand was clasping the shattered stump where his right arm had been severed just below the elbow. Dark gore was still gouting between his fingers and spreading in a black pool about his outthrust legs. Most dreadful was a great gash in his side from which protruded a glistening dark mass which must have been his liver. Above this wreckage, his eyes were large and luminous in a young man's face, pallid to the point of translucency.

"Vasser... please giff... vasser."

Reluctantly I shook my head. "Sorry, chum, I've got none. Nein vasser. Only rum, and that's no good for you."

The eyes, so vividly alive in the dying body, pleaded with me. Oh, hell, I thought, he's going anyway. What harm!

I held the water bottle to his lips and he swallowed in deep, spasmodic gulps until I took it back and drank from it myself. And so... and so the two of us got drunk together. And in a little while he died.

Some time later I found the tanks and managed to hang on to the turret of one of them on the ride back to where Baker Company was forming up to launch a new attack. I remember sliding off the front of the Sherman, and my legs collapsing under me, then there was nothing.

WHEN I WOKE it was morning of the day before Christmas. I was lying on a straw pallet in a corner of a lamp-lit room with vaulted stone ceilings. The place was crowded with sodden and exhausted men, including several company commanders and their radio operators. An O-group was in progress. Once again Doc was shaking my shoulder.

"Colonel says ya gotta get up, boss," he told me sternly. Then his broad face lightened. "Here... see what I got for ya! Pair of clean socks. Liberated 'em out of a dead Jerry's kit."

He was as pleased with himself as if he had brought me a captain's promotion, and he had reason to be, for clean, dry socks had become only distant memories to us in that time and place. I pulled them on and was astonished at how good they made me feel.

I found Kennedy in the next room pointing out something on a map to the company commanders. I listened with a feeling of detachment as he briefed them, but I remained keenly aware of my new socks and I scrunched my toes in them with exquisite pleasure.

The battle had raged all night and was still raging. The rifle companies were only just managing to cling to the mile-long salient which we had rammed through the German defence line; and now we were running out of men. Able was reduced to little more than platoon strength and the other companies were hardly better off. Although a few replacement officers had reached us, we had received no reinforcement drafts of other ranks since early in November.

Kennedy looked up at me from deeply sunken eyes. His voice sounded inexpressibly weary, lacking the bark and bite with which I was so familiar.

"A draft's arrived at San Vito. Supposed to come up tomorrow. I want them here tonight. Go and get them, Squib, and don't let anything or anybody stand in your way."

My fury had long since evaporated ... and nothing had yet taken its place. My thoughts were still chiefly concerned with my new socks as I pulled on my Castropignano blanket coat and stepped outside. Then it all came back upon me with the smothering impact of an avalanche.

I had emerged into a haze of driven sleet sweeping across a blasted landscape, most of whose inhabitants were huddling unseen in flooded slit trenches or in the gaping ruins of crumbled buildings, like dumb and enduring beasts passively awaiting what was yet to come. The relentless rains and incessant bombardment had turned the whole achromatic wasteland into one enormous wallow through which no mechanical transport, not even the ubiquitous jeeps, could pass. The only movement came from little groups of mules and men laden with food and ammunition, sloshing along tracks that were more like running rivers. Tiny, indistinct figures in a void, men and mules plunged half-drowning into the roadside ditches as new storms of shellfire lashed over them.

A world of shadows, of primordial gloom, of inchoate violence, lay around me ... *and no birds sang.* Memory jarred convulsively: *O what can ail thee, Knight at arms,/Alone and palely loitering?/The sedge has withered from the Lake,/And no birds sing!* ... A moment's respite in the time that was, then I was staring down a vertiginous tunnel where all was dark and bloody and the great wind of ultimate desolation howled and hungered. I was alone ... relentlessly alone in a world I never knew.

Shaking as if in the grip of a malarial attack, I stumbled back into the building where our new medical officer, a young Syrian named Homer Eshoo, was organizing a stretcher party to carry half a dozen badly wounded men to the rear. Homer gave me a casual glance, looked at me more closely, then came quickly to me. He thrust a mess tin of rum into my hands and let me drink deeply of it before pushing me toward the door. Not a word passed between us, but we both knew.

I walked out of the salient like a disembodied spirit. Presumably there was shellfire, but I do not recall it. My perceptions were not clouded by alcohol but by a mutiny within—by the withdrawal of sensation. I walked in the silence within myself, hearing nothing but an echo of the great wind...

On the south side of the Moro I was picked up by the driver of the commanding officer's jeep. Halfway to San Vito the little car splattered up to a marching column. It was our reinforcement draft on its own way forward, led and impelled by Alex Campbell—Major Campbell now—returning to us from hospital in North Africa.

Alex was striding along like a colossus of old: huge, indomitable, indestructible. When he saw me he gave a great, fond shout of recognition and pulled me out of the jeep into a bear hug. And I hugged him back so desperately and unashamedly that he too must have known.

"Farley!" he cried, his heavy hand on my shoulder. "Still here? And not a general yet? Must be all that verse you write. Bad for promotion. Here, I've been versifying too. Read this when you get time, and tell me what you think."

He pulled an envelope out of his battledress jacket and handed it to me. I tucked it away unread and fell in beside him as the column marched on, and I was like someone brought back to the surface from an abyssal deep... brought to the surface, but with no shore in sight.

Alex told me that the hundred and forty soldiers following us had arrived in England from Canada only a month earlier.

231

Inadequately trained and unprepared for what awaited them, they had been prematurely shipped to Italy to transfuse our wasted regiment. Marching behind us in their clean, new uniforms, they joked with one another, stared curiously at the debris of war, and sang the brave and foolish songs they had learned in Canada.

The singing faltered as we crossed the Moro and climbed up through the chaos of destruction which was what remained of San Leonardo. It ceased altogether as we entered the salient and passed thirty or forty of 3rd Brigade's fatal casualties stacked like cordwood by the shattered road where they had been placed to keep them out of the muck... until they could be housed in it permanently.

The first warning shells fell close at hand and Alex shouted an order to increase the interval between men to five yards. It was not enough. A few minutes later we were enveloped in a brief but murderous bombardment from 15-cm howitzers. Before it ended, seven of these newcomers to our inferno were dead or wounded. As for the rest, their education had been well begun.

During my absence Battalion Headquarters had moved farther forward and I reported to Kennedy in what had once been a large and prosperous farmhouse. In addition to ourselves, it was giving precarious shelter to several peasant families whose homes had already been destroyed. However, there was not room for all of us, and so my next task was to get these refugees started toward the rear.

Passively they allowed themselves to be herded out into the storm of rain and steel, encumbered by their babies, bundles and even some wicker baskets full of sodden hens. There was no resistance except from a tall, bent patriarch who, I believe, must have been blind. He sat in a weighty, carved wooden chair, his hands clutching the ornate arms with such strength and tenacity that we would perhaps have had to break his bony fingers in order to release his grip. His aged body trembled violently but he would not be persuaded, and could not be forced to leave.

"Says he was born here," our interpreter told me. "His father's fathers were born here. His children were born here. And the old son of a bitch says he won't leave unless the *Pope* tells him to!"

So the old man stayed to share our Christmas Eve.

In the rain-drenched darkness of that night the Royal Canadian Regiment moved up into the salient to launch an attack. Their intelligence officer came to get the form from me and we stood together in the shelter of a deep, stone doorway watching the infantrymen plod by—a wavering and serpentine frieze of phantasmagoric figures, rain-soaked and black as the night itself. The shelling began again and before I fled to the farm's cavernous wine cellar I saw those dim shapes sinking down into the slime as if they were earth spirits returning whence they came.

The RCR did not—could not—attack. No more could we; but there was to be no peace on Christmas Eve. All night long paratroop patrols fought to penetrate the salient, and the enraged whicker of automatic small arms and the muffled thud of bursting grenades seemed to echo everywhere in a blind confusion of vicious little battles.

Big guns of both sides sought to intervene and the wild, wet night glared with bursts of flame and reverberated to the clangour of explosions. Direct hits on the farmhouse brought heavy roof tiles hailing down and opened the upper storeys to an icy blast of wind and rain; but the massive lower walls remained intact and so did the vaulted cellar which now sheltered both the aid post and the I-section, and where I waited for the interminable night to end.

Silent and immobile against the curves of dimly seen wine vats, the old Italian farmer also sat and waited, his dull gaze staring into emptiness. I cannot guess what apprehensions filled his thoughts, but mine were laden with a corrosive dread that Kennedy might order me out of my burrow to take a message to one of the forward companies. I was convinced that if he did, *and if I went* (such was now the magnitude of my fear that it might, paradoxically, have given me the courage to refuse), there would be no return. I could tolerate no greater weight of terror. I knew I would act as the two nameless friends my father had written about had acted in the dark and distant hour of an earlier war.

Black, nauseous dread was the burden of that livid night. After a time I remembered the poem Alex had given me to read; and in an attempt to escape from the abyss, I fished it out of my tunic. It was scrawled in pencil on a soiled sheet of Salvation Army canteen paper and his angular script was difficult to read in the shaky light of a kerosene lantern that jumped and flared whenever a shell exploded near at hand.

When neath the rumble of the guns
I lead my men against the Huns,
I am alone, and weak, and scared
And wonder how I ever dared
Accept the task of leading them.
I wonder, worry, then I pray:
Oh God, who takes men's pain away,

Now, in my spirit's fight with fear,
Draw near, dear God, draw near, draw near!
Make me more willing to obey,
Help me to merit my command.
And if this be my fatal day,
Reach out, oh God, thy helping hand.
These men of mine must never know
How much afraid I really am!
Help me to stand against the foe,
So they will say: He was a man!

How much afraid I really am! I had not known... had not even suspected. That scatheless pillar of a man... and yet, the Worm was in him too!

There was no comfort for me in that shattering discovery. With something akin to revulsion I stuffed the poem back into my pocket as Corporal Castle appeared with a message in his hand. It was a cypher from Brigade and, with inexpressible relief, I immersed myself in the mundane task of decoding it. Then someone brought around a canister of hot tea. Two German prisoners were brought in to be searched. The explosion of a shell in one of the upper rooms set the dust dancing so thickly that for a time the lamp was only a dim, red glow in a grey murk. Once I tried to sleep in a filthy little funk-hole under a collapsed stairway, but the Worm was there and drove me out of it. Homer Eshoo, who had been tending the wounded almost without a break since the battle began, found a few free moments to share a drink with me... The hours eroded as slowly as granite, but brought no summons to send me out into the sounding night.

Dawn came at last, and it was Christmas Day.

And at 0700 hours Kennedy ordered Able Company to attack and destroy a force of paratroopers that had infiltrated during the night between Able and Baker. Kennedy himself went forward to give Alex his instructions... and this time he did not take me with him.

I tried to follow the course of the action through the earphones of the radio set connecting us with Able Company, but Able's set went off the air and I knew little of what was happening until half an hour later the walking wounded began to straggle into our cellar.

One of the first was a sergeant who was suffering from a deep gash in one thigh. Shakily he accepted a cigarette, then told me what he had seen.

Alex had sent what was left of Seven Platoon to launch the initial attack, and Seven had almost immediately been caught by enfilading fire from three machine guns, with the loss of several killed and wounded. The logical course would then have been for Alex to send one of the other platoons to outflank these guns (something that was successfully done later in the day) but he did not choose to do this. Instead he did the unexpected and the inexplicable.

Seizing a Tommy gun he levered his great bulk to its full height, gave an inarticulate bellow, and charged straight at the enemy.

He could have gone no more than three or four paces before he was riddled by scores of bullets. Crashing into the mud like a falling colossus, he lay there, his body jerking spasmodically until the dead flesh at last lay still. During that timeless interval, both his own men and the Germans were so stunned by his action that not a further shot was fired by either side.

"It was the bravest goddamn thing I ever saw... and the craziest!" The sergeant ground out his cigarette and looked into my face with puzzled eyes. "Crazy as hell! But Jesus, what a man!"

THE BLANKET THAT screened the shattered cellar door was thrust aside and a party of stretcher-bearers pushed in amongst us. Al Park lay on one of the stretchers. He was alive, though barely so... unconscious, with a bullet in his head.

As I looked down at his faded, empty face under its crown of crimson bandages, I began to weep.

I wonder now... were my tears for Alex and Al and all the others who had gone and who were yet to go?

Or was I weeping for myself... and those who would remain?

ACKNOWLEDGEMENTS

"THIRD YPRES" BY EDMUND BLUNDEN reprinted from *Undertones of War* by Edmund Blunden, London: Collins, 1965; "Fragment" by Rupert Brooke reprinted from *Collected Poems*, New York: Dodd, Mead and Company, 1941, and Toronto: McClelland & Stewart; "Recalling War" by Robert Graves reprinted from *Collected Poems*, London: Cassell & Company, 1959. The verse on page 230 is from "La Belle Dame Sans Merci" by John Keats.

THE DOUGLAS & MCINTYRE
FARLEY MOWAT LIBRARY

People of the Deer

A Whale for the Killing

And No Birds Sang

Sea of Slaughter

Born Naked

The Snow Walker

Please visit www.douglas-mcintyre.com
for upcoming titles in this series.

FARLEY MOWAT (1921-2014) began writing upon his return from serving in World War II and wrote 44 books, which have sold nearly 25 million copies in more than 60 countries. He spent much of his youth in Saskatoon and lived in Ontario, Cape Breton and Newfoundland, while traveling frequently to Canada's far north. Throughout, Mowat remained a determined environmentalist, despairing at the ceaseless work of human cruelty. His ability to capture the tragic comedy of life on earth has made him a national treasure in Canada and a beloved storyteller to readers around the world.